AUSTRALIA'S FIRST
ONLINE COMMUNITY
IPSWICH QUEENSLAND

AUSTRALIA'S FIRST ONLINE COMMUNITY IPSWICH QUEENSLAND

A CASE STUDY IN INNOVATION AND REGIONAL ECONOMIC DEVELOPMENT

MAL BRYCE

To order additional copies of this book, contact:
Xlibris Corporation
1-800-618-969
www.xlibris.com.au
Orders@xlibris.com.au
500448

CONTENTS

Part 6—The Timeline

Part 7—References

Part 8—Appendices

Index

To Sean, Katrina, Fiona, and Samantha who remained at home in Perth during five very important years of their lives, and to my wife, Liz, who made a valuable contribution to the Ipswich community in her own right as a foundation staff member of the West Moreton Anglican College, 1994-7

A Note from the Author

Most of my career in both the public and private sectors has been devoted to harnessing the power of new technology for the development of companies, communities, educational institutions, and governments.

One of the most exciting and creative chapters of that career was the five years I spent in Ipswich and Brisbane in Queensland, Australia, 1992-97.

On more occasions than I can possibly recall, I have been asked, 'Why Ipswich?' The answer in short is that when I met the leadership (the mayor, the general manager, and the chairman of the Economic Development Committee) of the city of Ipswich for the first time on 6 August 1992, I discovered that they were single-mindedly determined to embark upon an economic turnaround strategy for the city.

In the late 1980s and early 1990s, with the closure of many of its traditional industries, Ipswich had become a well-recognised epicentre of unemployment in Australia. The city's leaders wanted someone to develop and implement an economic development program for the city. When I outlined my approach to the task, they warmed to my enthusiasm for a strategy which included a commitment to information technology-led economic development. They offered me the challenge, and I accepted.

In my capacity as corporate manager for development investment (1992-6) I had the privilege to lead the team that conceived, designed, and built Australia's first online community as a catalyst for innovation and economic development. In 1997, I worked as a consultant to the vice-chancellor of the University of Queensland to help design the scope and nature of the new university campus to be established in Ipswich.

When we pressed the button and went live with Ipswich Global Info-Links on 8 December 1994, no fewer than fifty people had participated in creating what was a rather unique innovation in world terms.

We had begun to harness the power and potential of the Internet in order to build an information-rich community. Together with the university project, we had laid the foundations for Ipswich to take its place with pride in the Knowledge Economy of the twenty-first century.

For me personally, it was the privilege of a lifetime to lead a highly creative team whose work helped open so many different doors for a dynamic community, which at the time had its back to the wall.

Message from the Mayor of Ipswich

The idea of local government getting involved in telecommunications was first floated in the early 1990s when Ipswich's traditional industries were in decline.

As a newly elected councillor at the time, it was important to acknowledge that the world was changing, the city was changing, and we needed to look to a future based on technology and education.

All councils were primarily concerned with roads, rates, and rubbish, but if Ipswich was to grow, prosper, and reinvent itself, a fundamental shift in thinking was needed.

Ipswich City Council's chief executive officer during this period was Jamie Quinn who assisted greatly in realising the vision of Global Info-Links.

It didn't happen easily, but council's decision to establish Global Info-Links and to provide 125 schools with a dial-up Internet connection was critical to getting students interested in not only computers, but the wider Internet, and all it offered.

Seniors also took to the brave new world of the Internet as Ipswich also pioneered SeniorNet to assist older residents learn computer and Internet skills.

The city would be a very different place today if council had not persisted with establishing an ISP at a time when an email address was a novelty and a dialup connection considered state of the art.

The modernisation of the image of Ipswich was assisted to a large extent by Global Info-Links. This led to the establishment of not one, but two university campuses in the city.

The rest of the GIL story unfolds in the following pages.

On behalf of the city, I congratulate Mal Bryce on documenting an important chapter in the history of Ipswich.

Mayor Paul Pisasale
City of Ipswich

November 2010

Acknowledgements

Our rather audacious commitment to turn Ipswich into one of the world's first online communities in the early 1990s occurred when Australia and the world were undergoing widespread constant change. At that time it was not a simple matter to understand what was happening to commercial systems and community institutions.

I am indebted to many professional friends with whom I conducted a dialogue over more than twenty years in an endeavour to understand the shape of things to come as the ICT revolution produced so many challenges to the status quo. Coming to grips with a world in a constant state of flux made for exciting albeit frustrating times. To Bernard Stapleton, John Phillimore, Paul Houghton, Helen Clancy, Brian Haines, Larry Quick, Phil Deschamp, Earl White, John Syme, Peter Morris, Richard Naylor, Jamie Quinn, Neil McPhillips, Rob Cook, Ron Johnston, John Barker, Gerry Freed, and Peter Kenyon—I thank you for your patience, your opinions, and your insights.

During the last few months of 2008, I personally interviewed eighteen people who had been directly involved in the 1990s with the implementation of the Ipswich city's original economic development program. I am grateful to them for making their time available. Without their assistance I could never have plugged so many gaps in my own memory.

The shape of the original manuscript benefited significantly from valuable feedback I received from John Phillimore, Helen Clancy, Jamie Quinn, Quentin Beresford, Bernard Stapleton, Brian Haines, and John Barker.

I also gratefully acknowledge the assistance of Lyn O'Leary, Leanne Sherriff, Laurie Mundt, Narelle Rhodes, Cathy Watson at the Ipswich City Council as well as Andrea Druyan at Curtin University, and Professor Alan Rix at the University of Queensland, Ipswich Campus, in providing me with contemporary information and helping me to assemble the manuscript. Lyle Radford and the Queensland Times also generously supplied photographs for the project.

I will always be deeply indebted to all my former workmates at the Ipswich City Council during the early and mid-1990s for the privilege of being able to pioneer with them at a time when no one, anywhere in the world, had all the answers.

Preface

The last eighteen years (1992-2010) has been a period of remarkable transformation for the city of Ipswich in Queensland, Australia. What has happened in Ipswich is a case study in Innovation and Regional Economic Development applied especially to turnaround and renewal. For almost twenty years prior to 1992, Ipswich, like numerous other proud industrial cities around the world, had gone into a tailspin of economic and social decline. The period covered in this book (1992-7) constitutes a classic tale of turnaround. Serious renewal and transformation has occurred in the thirteen years following 1997.

Neither the turnaround years nor the renewal era happened by accident. Both of these chapters in the history of the city involved a very special generation of professionals who provided the city's political leadership and management. Both eras involved the development and implementation of detailed strategies.

This success story involved intervention by the Ipswich City Council after two decades (the 1970s and 1980s) of market failure in solving the problems of the city. The intervention provided vision, infrastructure, talented people, careful management, adequate financial resources, and a quite extraordinary level of belief and energy. Above all, it involved real courage.

By the end of the 1980s, the city faced a serious threat to its viability. This amounted to a challenge of the highest order. The challenge produced a response led by the Ipswich City Council, and the direct outcomes arising from that response have had a major impact on the long-term future of the city.

At a time when city councils were not well known for their economic development programs or their reputations as innovators, the city of Ipswich embarked upon a range of wholesale innovation. Ipswich city fundamentally transformed its system of administration and management in 1992 just prior to embarking on a creative strategy to arrest the decline of its local economy and turn around its prospects for the future. That economic turnaround strategy contained within it a particular commitment to embrace the concept of IT-led economic development.

The decision of the Ipswich City Council to network all households, businesses, community organisations, and government agencies, and connect them to the outside world via a phenomenon called the Internet in 1993, amounted to a serious world-class innovation. This was not innovation for improvement of what already existed. It was not innovation via evolution but innovation, which amounted to a gigantic leap forward from a position outside the box.

Virtually no one had heard of the Internet or its extraordinary potential in 1992/3. Facing an imperative to find alternatives to traditional economic activity, the city of Ipswich seized the window of opportunity that presented itself and became one of the world's earliest adopters of a technology that has transformed the operation of business, entertainment, government, and the professions since the mid-1990s. The success of the Global Info-Links project that turned Ipswich into one of the world's first online communities earned Ipswich a reputation for resilience and innovation. Amongst many other tangible outcomes the project provided a rallying point at a crucial time when hope and vision was needed.

Part 1 identifies the challenge.
Chapter One is a thumbnail sketch of the city of Ipswich in the context of the industrial revolution in Australia and describes the nature of the threat to its existence as a home for 80,000 people. Chapter Two examines the concept of IT-led economic development which was a relatively new concept in Australia in the late 1980s and early 1990s. Reference is made in this chapter to the Long Wave Theory of Economic Development in a way that puts the ICT revolution into an historical context.

Part 2 describes the response to the challenge.
Chapter Three provides a summary of the seven-point economic development program which was implemented as an economic turnaround strategy. Chapter Four amounts to a brief history of the evolution of the Internet phenomenon both internationally and within Australia. Chapter Five deals with the definition of the online community and draws the distinction between geographic communities (communities of location) and virtual communities (communities of interest and practice). Chapter Six deals with the origins and express purpose of the Global Info-Links project which saw the Ipswich City Council establish one of Australia's most successful ISPs in the mid-1990s. Chapter Seven outlines some of the many trials and challenges associated with building and operating an Internet Service Provider in the early 1990s.

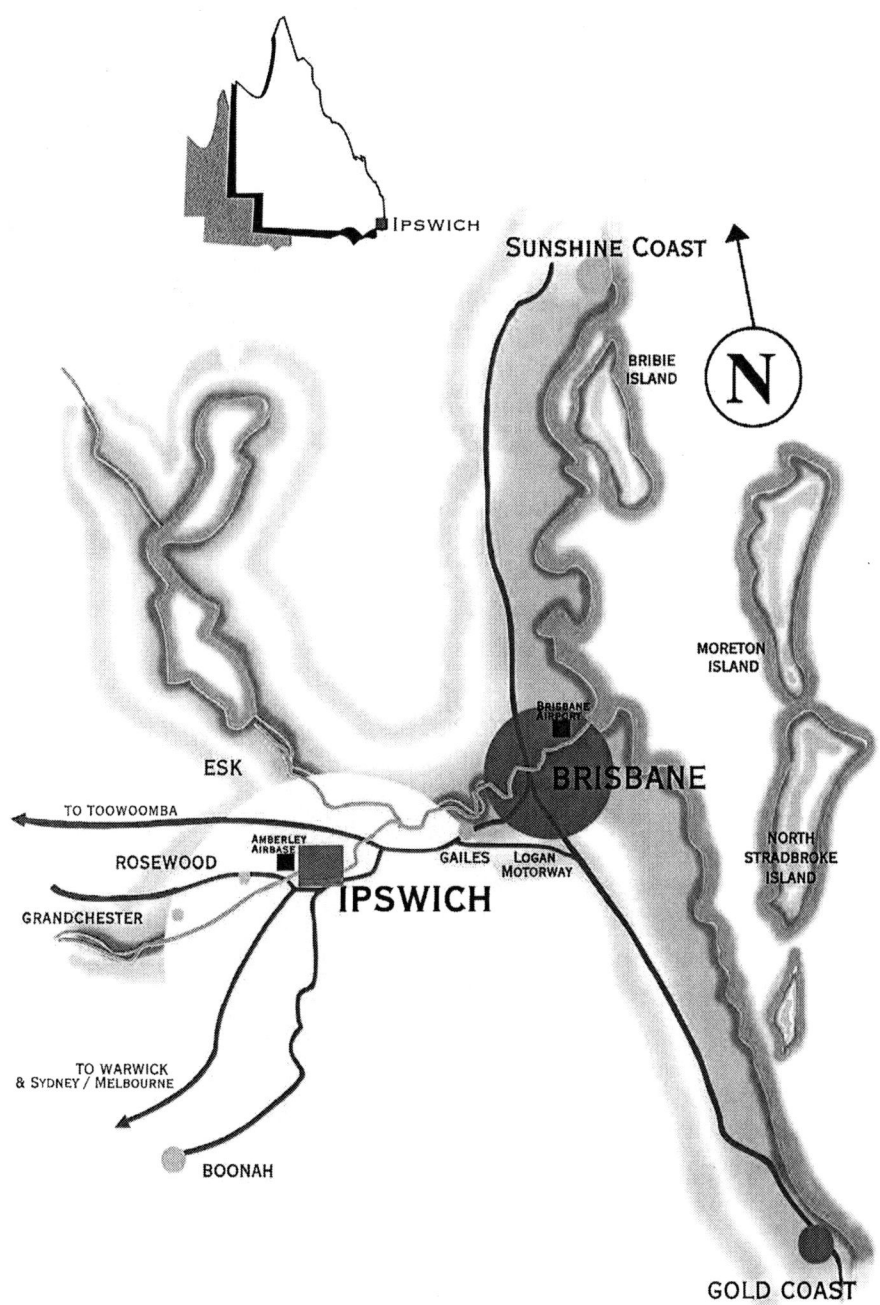

IPSWICH

SUNSHINE COAST

BRIBIE
ISLAND

N

MORETON
ISLAND

ESK

TO TOOWOOMBA

AMBERLEY
AIRBASE

ROSEWOOD

GAILES   LOGAN
MOTORWAY

BRISBANE
AIRPORT

BRISBANE

NORTH
STRADBROKE
ISLAND

IPSWICH

GRANDCHESTER

TO WARWICK
& SYDNEY / MELBOURNE

BOONAH

GOLD COAST

Ipswich location map

Part 3 identifies a number of tangible outcomes.

Chapter Eight describes some of the many assumptions we made in the early days of our journey to connect the households, businesses, and community organisations of Ipswich to the information highways of the world. It also provides an understanding for the observer outside Ipswich of the various stages in the life of Global Info-Links. Chapter Nine highlights the key features and significance of establishing a world-class Library Information Service in the city of Ipswich in 1995. Chapter Ten describes what we called the 'education module' and explains what it meant to be the first community in Australia to connect all private and public schools in our region to the Internet for the first time. Chapter Eleven discusses the origins, nature, and purpose of Ipswich SeniorNet, which was one of our most treasured innovations associated with the online community project. Chapter Twelve outlines what our objectives were with the 'business module' of the project and describes some of the very earliest endeavours to establish eCommerce in Australia. Chapter Thirteen, albeit without an actual screen grab of the original Ipswich/GIL homepage, describes what Australia's first community web site contained when it went live in 1994. Chapter Fourteen is a cameo of the journey often described as the twin project to Global Info-Links, which was the project to establish a university campus in Ipswich. These two projects together formed the backbone of the turnaround strategy for Ipswich. Within the Ipswich City Council the projects were developed and implemented simultaneously by basically the same team of people.

Part 4 peers into the future.

Chapter Fifteen examines the concept of the 2009 plan for Ipswich InfoCity and considers some of the implications of the broadband economy in the years ahead.

Part 5 presents some interesting conclusions.

Chapter Sixteen attempts to provide an answer to the question which is so often asked—Why did it happen in Ipswich in 1992-7? Chapter Seventeen outlines the transformation of the city of Ipswich which has occurred since the implementation of the turnaround strategy in 1992-7.

Part 6 provides a timeline from 1991 to 2001.

This comprises a summary of the key events as they occurred with the twin projects to establish both Global Info-Links and a campus of the University of Queensland in Ipswich.

In 1993, the Ipswich City Council as a local governing authority began to drive what was one of the first serious local economic development strategies in Australia. The original strategy was subsequently enhanced and extended and finally superseded. The latest version of the Ipswich Economic Development Strategy is the Ipswich City Council's vision for the next twenty-two years, 2009-31.

The thirteen years following 1997 have produced sustained high levels of exciting development. In 2010, the city is on the cusp of greatness again. It has become the engine room for the growth of South East Queensland, one of Australia's (and the world's) most prosperous and rapidly expanding regions.

PART 1

THE CHALLENGE

- Economic Downturn in the City of Ipswich
- Information Technology-Led Economic Development

Economic Downturn in the City of Ipswich

'. . . In 1993 we decided to head down a new pathway for our community and businesses. To waterways, rubbish ways, roadways and driveways we added information highways . . .'

Paul Pisasale, Mayor of Ipswich and long-standing Chair of Ipswich
City Council Economic Development Committee.
11 September 2008

Australia's industrial revolution in the late nineteenth and early twentieth centuries occurred in six state capital cities and eight regional cities. Those key regional cities in the twentieth century were Newcastle and Wollongong in New South Wales, Geelong in Victoria, Whyalla in South Australia, and Ipswich in Queensland, together with the three large integrated inland mining centres—Broken Hill (NSW), Kalgoorlie (WA), and Mt Isa (QLD). Other great mining centres emerged in Western Australia and Queensland in the last quarter of the twentieth century, associated with a new era of extensive open-cut mining for iron ore, coal, bauxite, and nickel.

The city of Ipswich is situated just forty-five kilometres due west of Brisbane and was for more than a century the heartland of heavy industry in Queensland. Queensland's economy has traditionally been the third largest state economy in Australia after the states of New South Wales and Victoria. In internationally comparative terms, during the nineteenth and twentieth centuries, Queensland was to Australia what Alberta was to Canada and essentially what Texas was to the USA, with some differences in the types of fossil fuels.

Ipswich at the end of the first decade of the twenty-first century is now a highly diversified, thriving growth centre for South East Queensland. It is centrally located in the booming south-east corner of the state. To the east is the capital city, Brisbane, and to the west are the rural and agricultural areas of the Brisbane, Lockyer, and Fassifern Valleys. The city is strategically positioned on the national road network—a forty-minute drive from Brisbane, an hour's drive from the Gold Coast, and slightly more than an hour's drive from domestic and international air and sea ports.

Modern Ipswich comprises an area of 1,090 square kilometres and has a population of 160,000 people. The city enjoys a subtropical climate and is proud of its multicultural tradition. The residents of the city come from 115 different ethnic backgrounds, speaking eighty-four languages.

After very early economic activity in the 1820s and 1830s to extract limestone for building and construction work in Moreton Bay, Ipswich was actually founded in 1842. For the next 130 years Ipswich developed as one of the world's classic integrated mining and industrial cities based on coal mining, heavy engineering and steel fabrication, the supply of building materials, a major rail service and maintenance centre, power generation, abattoirs, and textile mills. The highlights of Ipswich's economic development as an industrial centre read like a catalogue of the industrial revolution.

- 1820s and 1830s: A limestone-extraction industry attracted interest in the locality which became Ipswich.
- 1842: Ipswich was formally established as a free settlement.
- 1840s: Saw the beginnings of the coal mining industry (essentially deep mining).
- 1860: Ipswich officially became a municipality.
- 1863: Queensland's first secondary school (Ipswich Grammar School) was opened.
- 1860s: Queensland's first railway line from Ipswich to Grandchester was built (approximately 25 kilometres) and the Ipswich Railway Workshops were established.
- 1870s: The timber milling industry commenced in Ipswich and the first gas and coke companies were established. A pumped water supply to industry and households also began.
- 1890s: Cotton factories began operation.
- 1904: Ipswich was proclaimed a city.
- 1919: Public electricity was first supplied in Ipswich.
- 1930s: Woollen Mills were established in Ipswich.
- 1940s: Amberley Air Force Base was built and the Ipswich Railway Workshops played a major industrial supply/engineering role in World War II.
- 1950s and 1960s: Coal mining and heavy industry production reached their peak of output and importance.
- 1980s: Unemployment in Ipswich regularly exceeded 12 percent with wholesale closure of many mature secondary industries.

For the quarter of a century which followed the nineteen sixties, economic activity in Ipswich went into a tailspin of decline. A significant proportion of large enterprises which had previously been owned by local families were now owned and operated by national and international companies. The city experienced the pain of watching the sun set on many of its traditional industries which had enjoyed a proud past. One after the other, industrial firms downsized and eventually closed. The local economy and with it to a large extent the social fabric of the city unravelled during the nineteen seventies and eighties. By the early nineteen nineties Ipswich had become one of Australia's most recognised centres of long-term unemployment. General unemployment was nudging 13 per cent, and up to 25 percent of all youth were unemployed.

This phenomenon was of course occurring in numerous other industrial cities around the world, especially in Western Europe and North America.

Elsewhere in Australia during the nineteen eighties talk of the 'new economy' was just beginning, and there were many sceptics who expected the good old days of traditional secondary industry to return. Many industrial leaders and policy makers were firmly in denial that a paradigm shift in the economy was essential for the future.

In Canberra, the Hawke government had embarked upon a strategy of providing resources for Regional Economic Development, but not a great deal of attention was ever directed towards Ipswich.

Paul Keating as Treasurer was determined to make Australia globally competitive and deregulated exchange rates and interest rates. At the same time, the federal government embarked upon a vigorous program to reduce and eventually eliminate various forms of protection for Australian secondary industries. Many of those typical secondary industries were the backbone of Ipswich's local economy.

By 1990, although the image of Ipswich as a major mining and industrial centre persisted, there were actually more people in Ipswich employed in retailing than in the mining and secondary industries combined.[1]

The nearby capital city, Brisbane, was on the move and effectively achieved its introduction to the world with the hosting of 'The 1988 World Expo'. Ipswich on the other hand was at the back end of so many national statistics, such as unemployment, levels of income, criminal activity, and social security support.[2] The 1980s became the decade of strikes and industrial unrest especially in the mining, transport, power, and engineering industries.

---

[1] Interview with Bernard Stapleton (former Director of Deloittes), 10 September 2008, regarding the data on employment in Ipswich. Stapleton undertook the fundamental review of the Ipswich City Council's operations in 1992.

[2] Interview with Jamie Quinn, 9 September 2008, former CEO of the City of Ipswich (1989-2006)

In many respects, Ipswich, during this period, resembled a closed community isolated from the mainstream of economic investment and development. The people, although humble, were fiercely proud of their community and its organisations. In the midst of its darkest hour, in an economic sense, Ipswich continued to produce a string of Australia's Rugby League champions. It was the home of very proud working class traditions involving mutual support and fierce loyalty. However, to outsiders at the time, Ipswich was not regarded as a particularly attractive place to visit or in which to live.

Information Technology-Led Economic Development

> '... *Communities, states and companies which plan for the Information Age will be in a key position to reap its rewards* ...'
>
> (John Naisbitt, *Megatrends*, 1988)

In the early nineteen nineties the notion of information technology-led economic development was not exactly part of mainstream thinking for regional development in Australia.

During the last thirty years, with few exceptions, governments of all complexions at all levels (national, provincial, and local) in Australia have greatly underestimated the significance of the information technology sector of the economy. The industry has never been properly understood or recognised by policy makers and bureaucrats alike. At best, information technology as an economic phenomenon has simply been taken for granted.

Despite this the take up of the new technology in Australia has been surpassed by few other countries in the world. We have, however, tended to be the purchasers, users, and maintainers of other people's technology.

After riding on the sheep's back for almost two centuries, many Australians have found it difficult to look beyond 'rocks' and 'real estate' as the engines for economic growth. The decision of the Ipswich City Council in 1992/3 to embrace an IT-led economic development strategy constituted a significant break with tradition in terms of public policy.

For the sake of some clarity, a modicum of explanation concerning acronyms and terminology is probably helpful. Since the late 1970s, IT (Information Technology), IT&T (Information Technology and Telecommunications), and ICT (Information and Communications Technologies) are acronyms which have been widely used interchangeably to refer to the convergence of computing and telecommunications. Today, in addition to convergence, the evolution of whole new forms of media has popularised the use of ICT as the industry tag. In the early 1990s it was the IT Industry.

In conceptual terms there has always been a vertical and a horizontal dimension to the definition of the IT industry. The vertical dimension involves the traditional, somewhat narrow, definition of the IT industry as including those businesses whose main function is to produce hardware, software, and/or deliver services to install those IT products. This was the original IT revolution which followed the development and spread of the micro processor in the 1970s.

The horizontal dimension of the IT Industry takes into account the role of information technology as an enabling technology—a powerful set of tools that can be used in almost any industry and part of any strategy for economic and community development. In most countries of the world, the impact of IT as an enabling technology far exceeds the value and impact of the traditional hardware and software sectors. This was of major significance during the 1990s and the first decade of the twenty-first century.

Together with other information technology champions, I spent a great deal of time and effort in the 1980s trying to attract the so-called 'footloose' IT multinationals to establish plants in Australia. Policies to encourage the development of home-grown hardware and software companies were also produced in some parts of the nation. In many parts of the world (Australia included) this type of thinking led to the establishment of Technology Parks. However, by the 1990s the limitation of this approach to economic development was increasingly understood.

Our commitment to an IT-led economic development strategy in Ipswich was never intended to imitate or duplicate Silicon Valley in the Western Corridor of South East Queensland. Our express purpose was to achieve economic and community development by harnessing the power of telecommunications technology. We identified the Internet as the exciting new technology for that growth. After my early experience with the Internet in 1991/2, I had come to the conclusion that for the vast majority of the population, there was not much point in owning computers until they could talk to each other.

Developments in other parts of the world in the early 1990s had a significant impact on my view of the importance of IT-led economic strategies. In 1990, I undertook two missions with the United Nations into Czechoslovakia, designing policies to assist the development of the small business sector in what had been a command economy for forty-eight years. During visits to Geneva for these missions, I met key figures from developing countries who were pinning a great deal of faith in IT-led economic development strategies. In their eyes they felt they had discovered the means by which their economies could leapfrog the need to experience traditional industrialisation. In his report to the Asian Productivity Organisation in 1990,[3] Professor Tadao Saito of the Tokyo University defined IT-led economic development as

> '. . . a new type of development where Information Technology plays crucial roles in not merely accelerating the development process in a conventional sense, but in providing a new frontier of development possibilities . . .'

There was increasingly widespread belief that IT-led development was the avenue to enable developing countries to enter the information age. It was recognised that telecommunications infrastructure was as vital to the information age as other basic infrastructure such as electrical power, water, roads, and railways had been for industrial development.

Singapore is probably the world's most outstanding example of successful IT-led economic development. Singapore evolved from being a less developed nation to one of the world's most sophisticated marketplaces in less than twenty-five years. Their economic formula has been well documented, and it hinged on four key elements. Firstly, by leveraging its strategic location and establishing world-class transportation and materials handling facilities. Secondly, by establishing sophisticated communications and information technology systems. Thirdly, by continuously upgrading the skills of its workforce, and finally, by monitoring and absorbing relevant global technological developments as rapidly as possible.

Singapore recognised the strategic importance of information technology in the early 1980s. Its now famous National Computer Board was established in September 1981, and The Singapore National IT Plan was released in 1985 as an integrated strategy to fully exploit the potential of information technology in all sectors of the economy. The seven building blocks of the IT strategy were focussed on IT manpower, IT culture, IT infrastructure, IT application, IT industry development, a climate for creativity and entrepreneurship, and finally, coordination and collaboration.[4]

Since the early 1970s the information technology workshop of the world has traditionally been the United States of America. The growth of computing power and communications links in the 1970s and 1980s in the USA had been explosive. Throughout 1991 and 1992 President Bill Clinton and Vice President Al Gore had campaigned for the 1992 presidential election on the importance of the so-called Information Superhighways. The Clinton administration recognised that effective access to information via high-speed

---

[3]   A Report of the Asian Productivity Organisation on Information Technology. Nordica International Ltd, P 15, 1990.

[4]   IBID P229

communications links was a vital part of America's economic future. The technological challenge was not scientific—it lay in the understanding of the convergence in communications and computing technologies. The economic and political challenge was to secure support for the information systems that lay increasingly at the heart of all economic and social exchange.

Fifteen years on, Singapore is held up to the world as the exemplar of IT-led economic development for its sophisticated high-speed links and systems. In the US, the Clinton/ Gore ambition for their Information Superhighways has been mired in difficulty and complexity.

The massive level of investment in IT infrastructure on a global basis during the 1970s and 1980s probably rivalled in real terms the outlays for armaments in World War II. As a result our society and our economy were beginning to change in fundamental ways. International deregulation had occurred on a massive scale, freeing up trade, freeing up capital markets, and deregulating internal markets for goods and services. What amounted to a worldwide movement to deregulate and restructure the telecommunications industry in many respects became the leading example of global deregulation. Sadly for Australia while numerous other countries restructured their telecommunications carriers and moved on to invest heavily in the high-speed infrastructure for the broadband economy as a nation we have squabbled for more than a decade over who should own our national carrier and how it should be regulated.

The IT revolution which was well underway by the end of the 1980s was beginning to have a direct impact on how we learn, where and when we work, how we communicate, how we take our recreation, how we market, buy, and sell things, and how we organise our lives. This period of dramatic change also featured the emergence of new industries and organisations and the demise of many traditional organisational structures. None of us understood all the implications at the time, but we were experiencing a fundamental paradigm shift: from market place to market space, from passive media to interactive media and from closed networks to an Internet-worked world.

By the early 1990s the quality of telecommunications infrastructure had been identified as one of the critical criteria determining where and when corporations made decisions about relocating business activities or simply investing in new operations. Normally such decisions were determined by issues such as political stability, availability of skilled workforce, availability of raw materials, transport infrastructure and the cost of labour. In a survey of global corporations undertaken by the Gallop Group in 1994, the quality of telecommunications infrastructure appeared on this list for the first time. It was deemed to be the third most significant factor after political stability and skilled workforce. Economists were at the same time beginning to expand the sacred list of the factors of production to include information.

The reality was emerging that all the most wonderful supplies of land, labour, capital, and enterprise would not guarantee first-class success if information services were second rate.

The basis of the IT revolution of the 1980s was a matter of speed, cost reductions, energy requirements, miniaturisation, and reliability. The speed of calculation and recall improved at a phenomenal rate. Cost reductions were quite extraordinary and made it possible for small businesses, schools, and householders to own computers. Energy requirements were very low and the new wonder machines were economical to run. Large cumbersome mainframes in air-conditioned chambers were challenged by the arrival of PCs and laptops. The elimination of valves and wiring made computers virtually faultless.

The explosive growth of the telecommunications industry had been based on major technological innovation, deregulation, and globalisation of business. From 1985 to 1995 the volume of voice line activity around the globe had grown from 15 billion minutes to 60 billion minutes.[5] Of perhaps greater significance was the use of a global telecommunications system designed for voice traffic to transmit data. As a foundation plank of the digital revolution, in the USA in 1997 for the first time the volume of data traffic surpassed the volume of voice traffic. That happened in Australia in 1998.

The demise of distance as the key to the cost of communications turned out to be one of the most significant economic forces shaping the last twenty years. The cost of transmission became virtually independent of geography. The unit cost of transatlantic telephone traffic between 1960 and 1995 was a classic illustration.[6] In 1960, the estimated cost of a transatlantic telephone call was $US 4.60 per hour. By 1990 that cost was approximately seven cents per hour, and by 1995 it was approaching US1¢ per hour. It is interesting that charges for long distance calls remained in place for many years after this technological breakthrough.

Except in those parts of Australia mesmerised by the resource industry boom it was clear that revolutionary technological developments in IT were going to have a major impact on the shape of Australian society and the competitiveness of our economy.

If the sophisticated parts of the developing world and the world's leading super power had in the late 1980s and early 1990s embraced a serious IT-led economic development strategy for the future, it seemed to make eminently good sense to incorporate such an initiative in an economic turnaround strategy for a proud industrial city such as Ipswich. Ipswich was a city determined to play a key role in shaping its own future.

---

5   TAT Cables World Telecommunication Development Report, 1997.

6   IBID.

During the 1980s and 1990s the all embracing impact of the ICT revolution was recognised and writers and observers in many quarters began to describe what they were witnessing as a 'new economy'. There were tags aplenty. Initially the new economy was called the online economy, then the digital economy, the information economy, and subsequently the knowledge economy and even the creative economy. All these efforts were associated with an enthusiasm to describe the impact of the generation, manipulation, and distribution of massive volumes of information at great speeds over vast distances because of the new ICT infrastructure. Only time will tell how economic historians will best describe the period.

Experts who subscribe to the Long Wave Theory of Technological and Economic Development suggest that the last two hundred and fifty years of economic development have been largely determined by five long waves of development, each of approximately fifty to sixty years in duration. It is the view of this author that the world has just passed the half-way mark of the fifth great developmental revolution based on ICT and that high-capacity broadband will be the infrastructure that facilitates the full flowering of the ICT revolution in the next two or three decades.

Carlota Perez and her colleagues at SPRU (The Science and Technology Policy Research Unit) at the University of Sussex (UK) have probably done more than anyone to explain a clear and understandable view of the ICT revolution.

Perez is a champion of the Long Wave Theory of development, and in her latest book on the subject,[7] she points out with great expertise that the ICT revolution is the fifth great technological revolution to have determined the shape of the last two hundred and fifty years. Each of these great surges of economic development was based upon quite remarkable technological breakthroughs. Each of the surges lasted for more than fifty years. The first industrial revolution dates from 1771 with Arkwright's Mill. The second revolution (The Age of Steam and Railways) dates from 1829. The third revolution (The Age of Steel, Electricity, and Heavy Engineering) dates from 1875. The fourth revolution (The Age of Oil, Automobiles, and Mass Production) dates from 1908, and the fifth, which is the ICT revolution, dates from the release of the microprocessor in 1971.

Perez points out that each and every one of these revolutions has passed through four phases, two great periods, and a turning point:

- **Phase One (The Irruption Phase)** follows the big bang and the gestation period. It features new products, new industries, explosive growth, and fast innovation.

---

[7]   Carlota Perez. 'Technological Revolutions and Financial Capital', Edward Elgar, UK, 2005.

- **Phase Two (The Frenzy Phase)** delivers a full constellation of new industries, technologies, and systems associated with new infrastructure.

  These first two phases Perez describes as the installation period or first half of the revolution.

  In all five of the revolutions spanning more than two hundred years this period is capped off by a great bubble featuring manic behaviour and the inevitable crisis or crash.

  This causes a turning point which usually involves new forms of regulatory intervention by the state.

  The second main period of the revolution follows the turning point and is described by Perez as the deployment period comprised of phases three and four.

- **Phase Three (The Synergy Phase)** is characterised by a time for production, full expansion of innovation and market potential.

- **Phase Four (The Maturity Phase)** features the last of the new products and industries followed by market saturation (maturity) for many of the earlier products.

There is little doubt at the time of writing (2009) that we have reached the turning point of the ICT revolution. The world's financial systems are described in all quarters as being broken and discredited. Governments of the world are currently working on strategies to ensure that the excesses of the last five years 'never happen again'. The fundamental infrastructure for the next two phases of the ICT revolution (high-capacity broadband) is being rolled out and the foundations for the next great technological revolution are being laid. There is also little doubt that ICT technology is one of the vital keys to identifying, unlocking, and harnessing the awesome potential of the twenty-first century associated with nanotechnology, biotechnology, renewable energy, green chemistry, and regenerative medicine.

Global Info-Links as the engine for the Ipswich online community initiative was clearly a concept born at the end of phase one of the ICT revolution. For the project team that developed and managed Global Info-Links, the period from 1994 to 2000 was very much part of the era which follows the big bang and amounts to a gestation period featuring a vast range of new products, fast and constant innovation, new industries, and explosive growth.

PART 2

- An Economic Turnaround Strategy for Ipswich, 1992-7
- The Emergence of the Internet
- The Concept of the Online Community
- The Global Info-Links Initiative
- Building and Operating an ISP in the early 1990s

An Economic Turnaround Strategy for Ipswich 1992-7

'. . . Ipswich needed a catalyst. With IT-led economic development there was an explosion of ideas and thoughts which came together linking the library, the community and business to Information Technology . . .'

Bernard Stapleton: Co-founder of NBC Capital. Former Director of Management
Consulting for Deloittes Ross Tohmatsu. 10 September 2008

Local governments in Australia in the early 1990s did not have economic development committees or economic development managers nor did they have economic development plans and strategies. Economic development was generally deemed to be the preserve of federal and state governments and, of course, the private sector.

Local governments had traditional departments and time-honoured programs relating to engineering and works, planning, health, parks, and finance. The Ipswich City Council was one of the very first local government authorities in Australia to adopt strategic planning for the business of running a city and one of the earliest adopters of a serious commitment to economic development for the city. Faced with a devastated local economy, the Ipswich City Council resolved in 1992 that it was going to be proactively involved in the economic future of the city. With the support of the mayor (Dave Underwood) and the CEO (Jamie Quinn) at the time, the driver for this initiative was the indefatigable Councillor Pisasale. Paul Pisasale was elected Chairman of the Economic Development Committee of council in 1992, and although elected mayor in 2004, he still serves as Chair of that committee.

It is in the context of the first Economic Development Strategy for the city that the commitment to launch Global Info-Links and the concept of the online community was made. The Economic Development Strategy provided the operational program that developed the infrastructure and the services for Ipswich to become Australia's first online community.

Between 1991 and 1997 three very fundamental cultural changes swept through the Ipswich City Council that had a major bearing on its future and future of the city itself. The first two waves of cultural change were initiated from within the city, and the third was the result of external influences.

The first major cultural change (1992-3) was associated with the work done by Bernard Stapleton of Deloittes Ross Tohmatsu. As previously mentioned this work which was commissioned by the Ipswich City Council, restructured the city council's administration and operational wings. The council's priorities and style of management were modernised in very significant ways. Gone was the position of town clerk, replaced by a new corporate image associated with a leader called the general manager. Strategic planning was now the order of the day. Customer service had been discovered and was embraced as a program close to the heart of all city leaders. Ipswich City Council became a local government authority that was listening.

The second major cultural development (1993-5) was associated with the adoption of state-of-the-art information technology across all council departments, programs, and agencies. PCs arrived at everyone's work station, information systems were networked, a vast amount of staff training was undertaken, and in June 1993, the Ipswich City Council became Australia's first municipality to be connected to the Internet. Eighteen months later Ipswich launched Australia's (and one of the world's) very first local/community web site and gave birth to a new era of community consultation and communication for local government.

The third cultural experience (1995-7) was the implementation of the Queensland State Government's decision to merge the city of Ipswich with the neighbouring Moreton Shire Council. Although potentially debilitating when this move was announced, it ultimately proved to be of enormous benefit to the communities involved.

At the time of amalgamation Ipswich was a regional city with an urban population of approximately 80,000 people. The Moreton Shire, which virtually encircled Ipswich, had a population of approximately 50,000 people and was largely a rural community without a Central Business District. The two councils, especially after the restructuring of the Ipswich City Council in 1992/3, were culturally and administratively very different. The IT systems, the human relations systems, the staffing structure, and the fundamental management of the two entities were different in almost every respect. The merger election was held in early 1995 and the painstaking, time-consuming task of creating the new merged entity began. During this rather challenging time, the small team responsible for the Economic Development Strategy soldiered on with great support from the city's elected representatives, especially Councillor Paul Pisasale who had been re elected to council.

The distraction and disruption associated with the merger of the two local governing bodies lasted almost eighteen months. Today the new city of Ipswich covers an area of 1,090 square kilometres and has a population of 168,000 people with enormous potential for future growth.

Public policy associated with serious regional economic development initiatives emerged in Australia during the 1970s and 1980s. There had been ministries and departments for de-centralisation in various parts of the country during the 1950s and 1960s which had produced very little in terms of tangible outcomes. Mounting concern about the de-population of rural communities and the need to be more effective in planning the development of what was seen as bourgeoning capital city growth attracted the attention of governments across the political spectrum.

In the early 1970s the Whitlam government became the first Australian Federal Government to invest significant resources in regional development. The most high profile example of that era was the initiative in Albury-Wodonga on the border of New South Wales and Victoria. Ten years later in 1983, the Western Australian government launched the Bunbury 2000 Strategy which effectively revolutionised regional development in that state. Queensland itself had long been heralded as the most successfully de-centralised Australian state economy with an impressive list of bustling cities of more than 50,000 people outside the capital city. Ipswich, as the oldest city on that list in Queensland, was confronting serious problems by the late 1980s.

Throughout Australia, the key elements of most high-level strategies for regional development in the second half of the twentieth century involved identification of the following:

- ageing infrastructure which acted as an impediment to growth
- potential new components of the local economy
- key services that had simply never been provided

In practical terms this was usually translated into action to speed up the development approvals process, increase the supply of appropriate land, improve access to airports and other forms of public transport, deliver high quality contemporary health services, co-location and rationalisation of community facilities where duplication of effort was a problem, provision of modern post secondary education and training facilities and the de-centralisation of state and federal government departments and agencies. More intangible but by no means least important was the development of a local community psychology that welcomed and facilitated investment and development.

When it came to developing an economic turnaround strategy for Ipswich, considerable time and effort was spent analysing many interesting successes and failures in regional development during the previous two decades in Australia. The program which was adopted in 1993-6 included seven key components, some of which had interesting links to other rather high-profile chapters in the history of regional development in Australia. Some components of the strategy were brand new.

The program which was supported by the city's budget during the period 1992/3-96/7 included:

- **The information technology-led economic development strategy known as Global Info-Links**
  To give the city a competitive edge we were determined that Ipswich would be amongst the very early arrivals in the information age. Our declared mission was to make the Ipswich region an 'information rich community'. This involved electronically networking the city to harness the power of the Internet, providing universal access at reasonable cost, and improving government service delivery. To do this, we had to design, build, and operate our own Internet Service Provider (ISP). In Australia in 1993 commercial ISPs were only beginning to emerge. Those that existed were veranda or home-garage ventures. None were sufficiently robust, nor had the capacity to deliver what we required.

- **The design and construction of a new public library building/service**
  It seems strange to some observers that a new library service would be part of an economic development program. Our team suggested this initiative in early December 1992 as an integral part of an information links initiative. The city badly needed a dedicated library building. The result was a spectacular ($13 m) new building known as Ipswich Global Information Centre (IGIC). It was a great deal more than a traditional library service and was directly linked to the objective of providing universal access to highly contemporary information services for the people of Ipswich.

- **The establishment of a university campus in Ipswich**
  For more than a hundred years various people and newspaper editors had mooted the idea of a university for the city of Ipswich. The first concerted action to achieve this important objective occurred when it became part of the Ipswich City Council's Economic Development Program. On 10 December 1992, The Development Investment Group[8] suggested that council establish a University Taskforce for the

---

[8]   Ipswich City Council minutes incorporating a formal memo from the IDIM to the mayor, 10 December 1992.

express purpose of drawing up the case for establishing a university campus in the city of Ipswich. The first meeting of the taskforce was held on 3 February 1993.

On 10 December 1996, the University of Queensland publicly announced its decision to establish a campus in Ipswich. In June 1999, the Ipswich university campus of UQ was officially opened.

- **The redevelopment of the North Ipswich Railway Workshops**
  Ipswich had been a railway town since 1865, when Queensland's first railway line from Ipswich to Grandchester opened. During more than a century, the North Ipswich Railway Workshops were the maintenance/support hub for Queensland Rail, training and employing many thousands of tradesmen. By the 1980s Regional Development Strategies in many Australian towns were incorporating initiatives to re-locate railway stations, marshalling yards and workshops badly in need of modernisation. In many instances this infrastructure divided the town/city. The North Ipswich site was the Ipswich City Council's preferred site for the city's university campus until 1996 when the University of Queensland decided to establish its new campus at the Challinor Centre on the south side of the city. In the decade following 1996, the North Ipswich Workshop site has been re-developed and today incorporates an outstanding rail museum, the Riverlink retail shopping complex, and has provision for new inner city housing overlooking the Bremer River.

- **The modernisation and monitoring of Ipswich City Council's development approvals process**
  The speed and effectiveness with which applications for development are processed is often regarded as an indication of the enthusiasm of local and state government bodies for development. After its restructuring in 1992/3 the Ipswich City Council was determined to welcome investors to the city and substantially speeded up the process of achieving approvals for investment/development. Whilst the planning group of the council was responsible for the mechanics of the approval process, the development investment group was responsible for monitoring and reporting on the system.

- **The attraction of a major departmental store to the Ipswich CBD**
  The attractiveness and appeal of the central business district in the city of Ipswich had been a matter of concern to the Ipswich City Council for some decades. A significant number of modernisation and beautification program had been implemented in the late 1980s and early 1990s. The Ipswich Heritage Program had been an outstanding success in the early 1990s. Missing as a key element of downtown Ipswich was the presence of a major up-market department store. Over a three-year period, one by one all major department stores rejected our overtures to establish a store in the CBD. We were unable to convince them that the basic

demographic of Central Ipswich could support such a business. In a dramatic initiative in 2009 Ipswich City Council purchased a major component of the CBD with a view to modernising the precinct in a highly creative way and ultimately achieving this objective.

- **The establishment of a commercial airport facility in Ipswich**
  Primary responsibility for carriage of this issue rested with the Ipswich Regional Development Corporation (IRDC) but was keenly supported by the Ipswich City Council and its development investment group. The Corporation had a membership that involved four other neighbouring local governments with an eye on the future of the Western Corridor of South East Queensland. The nearest commercial airport in Brisbane was more than sixty kilometres away, and Ipswich was home to one of Australia's largest and most sophisticated defence airport facilities, the Royal Australian Air Force base at Amberley. Our objective was to replicate the model at Williamtown in NSW and Darwin in the Northern Territory to achieve a joint-use facility. Fifteen years later the Department of Defence remains less than enthusiastic about sharing the use of its infrastructure. As a result of the greatly increasing demand in the Western Corridor for a commercial airport facility, work has recently re-commenced to identify a dedicated site for a commercial airport in Ipswich.

These foundation stones of the Ipswich City Council's Economic Development Program of 1992-7 were subsequently expanded, modified, and enhanced in many ways in the years that followed.

The Emergence of the Internet

'. . . *Global Info-Links was right at the time for the Council to get involved in to provide our community with the Internet. It turned entire communities upside down in the ways people acquire information . . . the effect was so great that when you talk to people now it's hard to remember what it was like without it . . .*'

Paul Tully, Ipswich City Council Councillor since 1979. Long serving Chairman of the Ipswich City Council Finance Committee and the Planning and Development Committee
10 September 2008

The Internet has been a world-changing technology spawned in the second half of the twentieth century and destined to flower fully in the broadband age of the twenty-first century. Like the automobile, television, electricity, and the steam engine before it, the emergence of the Internet was characterised by a gestation period involving decades. The birth place and the primary engine room for the development of the Internet has been the United States of America.

The origins (late 1950s), the actual beginning (October 1969), and the serious take-off phase (1989-94) of the Internet unfolded over four decades. The hallmark of the fifteen years that has followed take-off has been explosive growth.

Actual gestation for the Internet really began in 1957 with the surprise launch of Sputnik, the world's first satellite by the Soviet Union. The Western world was stunned by this event. The late 1950s and early 1960s was one of the most dangerous periods of the Cold War which was to last for virtually forty-five years. On a daily basis almost, at that time, the world lived with the very real possibility of a nuclear holocaust. The USA responded to the launch of Sputnik with a series of important counter initiatives. Within just over a decade (July 1969) the US had landed the first man on the moon and in a much less heralded event had given birth to the Internet (September 1969).[9]

---

[9]   When the technological breakthrough at ARPANet made it possible to transmit bursts of data.

In Australia, the Menzies government's response to Sputnik was to find hundreds of millions of dollars for science facilities in the nation's secondary schools and universities. Around the world the US and its allies realised they had been caught napping by Soviet science and amidst widespread fear there was a single-minded determination to re-capture the lead.

In 1958, the Eisenhower Administration in the US established the Advanced Research Projects Agency (ARPA) to stimulate and manage brave new efforts in science and technology. As a high-profile former World War II military commander, Eisenhower was committed to minimising the prospects of future surprises.

After Sputnik, an immediate US priority for the new strategic initiatives was the nation's telecommunications systems. In the US there was great sensitivity about the vulnerability of their highly centralised civilian and military communications system. An important military objective for the US was henceforth to be able to survive and respond to a future surprise attack that would target amongst other things its traditional telecommunications infrastructure. Two key imperatives emerged. Firstly, to effectively decentralise the nation's communications systems, and secondly, to enable digital data as well as voice to be reliably transmitted via the networks.

The challenge of the 1960s was the development and refinement of 'packet switching' which breaks data into chunks or packets and lets each one take its own path to a destination. This phenomenon was the most basic of all building blocks for the Internet. The crucial hardware for sending and receiving bursts of data was developed in 1969 by Bolt, Berarek, and Newman for the Advanced Research Projects Agency. On 29 October 1969, the first data delivered on the Internet, called the ARPANet at that time, occurred between two host computers in the USA. One, at the University of California in Los Angeles, and the other, four hundred miles away at the Stanford Research Institute of Technology in San Francisco.

It took the next twenty-five years to develop the transmission protocols, hypertext, email, the World Wide Web, and a system of browsers and search engines to make the Internet as we know it today available to the population at large. The two vital protocols were the TCP (Transmission Control Protocol) and IP (the Internet Protocol). The TCP was designed in 1973 and the Internet protocol was developed in 1983 after which the network was referred to as the Internet. Throughout the 1980s the Internet expanded from 1,000 host computers in 1984 to 100,000 hosts in 1989.[10] The key to future explosive growth and success was the migration of the dozen or so US networks to the Internet protocol suite. In achieving this, a very fundamental standard had been established.

---

[10] At the time of writing (2009) there are more than 650 million host machines.

For the early adopters, reasons for connecting to the Internet were limited to certain rudimentary functions such as the following:

- transferring files between computers (1973)
- sending and receiving first generation email (1972)
- accessing bulletin boards (1980)

By 1990 in the US although the user base for the Net was more diverse, it was still basically restricted to early adopters such as universities, the military, software developers, computer scientists and technicians, and other research establishments. At this stage of its evolution, the Internet was still far from being user-friendly. It was slow, clunky, limited to green text on black screens, and not particularly reliable, i.e. subject to frequent dropouts and crashes.

Nineteen ninety-one proved to be a pivotal year for the Internet and mankind. Between 1990 and 1994 a succession of content provision, content discovery, and content access services were released.[11] Based on the work of Tim Berners-Lee and Robert Cailliau at one of the world's largest physics laboratories (CERN, Geneva, Switzerland), in 1991 the now famous World Wide Web was developed making it possible to link a vast number of documents in different locations. This effectively turned the Internet into the largest repository of information and knowledge in the history of mankind. To navigate this virtual ocean of information, instruments we call browsers and search engines were necessary. The very first user-friendly graphical interface to the Net was released to the world by Marc Andreessen in 1993 called Mosaic. Soon after Mosaic came Netscape (1994) and a multitude of others, including the Microsoft candidate, Internet Explorer, in 1995. A veritable kaleidoscope of search engines also followed. A browser is a program installed on a PC locally that is used to access the Internet, to view what is available. A search engine is a program that aggregates reference data so that when a user types in a phrase it can point that user in the direction of a web site that relates to the query. A browser is used to get to a search engine.

The first international link to ARPANet was established to University College in London via Norway in 1973. During the 1980s various other countries made connections to the USA usually led by computer scientists and technicians. In Australia, the military imperative did not drive the development of the Net. From the mid-1970s to the late 1980s, the Australian Computer Science Network developed as a private network for its members, which was not part of the Internet Protocol developed in the US. Not until 1988 was the initiative taken in Australia to establish a connection to the US-based Internet for all universities and the CSIRO. The Australian Vice-Chancellors' Committee in May 1989 approved the technical, financial, and business plans to establish the Australian

---

[11]   Roger Clarke 'Origins and Nature of the Internet in Australia', January 2004.

Academic and Research Network (AARNet). In June 1989, the connection between the University of Melbourne (as Australia's outlet/link to the world) and San Jose on the US west coast was established.

By May 1990, all Australian universities and the CSIRO were connected to AARNet, which was a purely IP network operated on a restricted access basis for the academic and research community. Access to the Internet by the general public or for commercial purposes, was simply not permitted. In this respect Australia closely followed the lead of the pioneers of the Internet in the USA.

In 1993, the Clinton administration changed the nature and the future of the Internet when it launched its National Information Infrastructure Initiative. That initiative virtually confirmed that in future not only would the network be available for commercial purposes, but that it would be funded and operated on a commercial basis. In Australia between 1989 and 1993 AARNet operated an Affiliated Membership program for commercial researchers, librarians, and a limited number of community groups. The Ipswich City Council in 1993 became the first local authority in Australia to gain access to the Internet through affiliate membership.

The general clamour for connection to the Net by organisations other than the research community placed demands on the budgets of universities and government research groups that could not be sustained. Eventually, the general usage policy had to change, and AARNet set in place (June 1994) what was called its 'Value Added Resellers Program'. Ipswich also became one of the very first value added resellers. During our planning and development phase for Global Info-Links (1993-4) Telecom as an organisation morphed into Telstra. It sounds quite difficult to believe all these years later, but we actually had to explain how to spell the word I-N-T-E-R-N-E-T to the operators of Australia's great telephone company in 1993. Their learning curve was dramatic and steep. By July 1995 such was pressure of demand for Internet services in Australia that the Australian Vice-Chancellors' Committee transferred all its commercial customers, associated assets, and the management of interstate and international links to the new Telstra. The era of the commercial ISP industry had arrived and the commercial and private use of the Internet in Australia never looked back.

As a world-changing technology, the Internet has been an extraordinary success because it made it possible for communities of people to communicate and interact quickly, inexpensively, easily, and broadly. In the words of Leonard Kleinrock[12] who was present at the moment of conception, the Internet today boasts a significant list of beneficial characteristics including:

---

[12]   L. Kleinrock :'The Internet Rules of Engagement: Then and Now', Computer Science Department, UCLA, 2004.

- no one controls it
- no one can turn it off
- it serves everyone
- it is an open network
- it provides a means to share works and ideas
- it is diversifying
- it is owned by no one
- it is empowering
- it is a publishing machine
- it offers a means of self-expression
- it is an innovation machine
- it is a marketplace of ideas, services, applications, and goods
- it connects communities of interest

This same visionary pointed out how mankind has been able to put the Internet to a whole host of negative uses, including the invasion of people's privacy, acting as a massive source of spam and junk, the generation and distribution of debilitating viruses, failure to obey the laws of many countries, and the spread of pornography.

The Concept of the Online Community

'. . . Suddenly Ipswich was in the media for a cutting edge, cognitive, thinking related initiative . . . the whole Smart City thing amounted to positive leadership . . . it was about a shift of the psyche in the Council and in education which linked schools to their community . . .'

Lindy McKeown, Australian Digital Futures Institute and former
teacher at Bundamba Primary School Ipswich.
12 September 2008

In the early 1990s the notion of an online community was virtually unheard of and certainly not recognised or understood by regional development practitioners. Community development prior to the emergence of the Internet focussed almost exclusively on geographical communities or communities of location. The evolution of Ipswich as an online community occurred in two phases.

The first phase involved Ipswich as a geographical community in 1994 providing the telecommunications infrastructure and services that gave its citizens networked access to people, data, and organisations worldwide. This online capability gave the people of Ipswich the means of communicating with each other, accessing information and expertise worldwide and the ability to promote their own community with unprecedented effectiveness.

The second phase followed soon after with the emergence of borderless communities of interest and practice. This enabled the citizens of Ipswich to join people in other parts of Australia and in numerous other parts of the world who shared a common, often passionate, interest in a large variety of different cultural, professional, political, and sporting activities.

At the end of the first decade of the twentieth century, the concept of community can therefore be thought of in spatial, organisational, and interest-based terms.

The word community is made up of three parts: com (with, together), munis (exchanges), and ity (intimate)—exchanges that link us together in an intimate fashion.

In the last twenty-five years, we have witnessed a paradigm shift from the manufacturing age to the age of knowledge and creativity. This paradigm shift has brought about some fundamental changes in the nature of communities. A large cross section of the world's people is feeling increasingly isolated and alienated from the physical communities in which they live. Many of those people yearn for a more inclusive society. Part of our purpose in Ipswich in 1993 was to address this general phenomenon.

When the Ipswich City Council connected to the Internet for the first time in June 1993 and subsequently delivered the Internet through 'Global Info-Links' to local households, schools, and businesses in December 1994, the city of Ipswich became Australia's first and one of the world's first online communities.

What made it feasible was the convergence of computing and telecommunications technologies during the 1980s and early 1990s capped off by several significant breakthroughs including the development of the World Wide Web in 1991. For the first time in the history of the world, it became possible for vast amounts of data and information to be collated and distributed over great distances at very fast speeds and very little cost. Families, businesses—large and small—community organisations, and government agencies could be effectively networked without massive investment. The world's telecommunications infrastructure which had been developed for voice traffic was now expected and called upon to transfer great volumes of data. That demand has grown exponentially since the late 1990s with the increased complexity and volume of data that businesses, householders, and community organisations have developed a thirst for.

In the decade that followed 1993/4 a great deal of emphasis was focussed on the cost of access, speed, and the reliability of the infrastructure. Eventually, the emphasis switched to developing a greater understanding of how the potential of the Internet world could be exploited.

What began as the concept of the online community took on an interesting variety of names, such as the digital community, the connected community, tele-community, the networked neighbourhood, the smart community, the intelligent community, and eventually, the creative and resilient communities. The first four in this list reflect a significant preoccupation with technology and infrastructure. The smart community concept and the vision for creative and resilient communities assume the existence of a modern technical and learning infrastructure and focus attention on the development of social capital and human creativity. This phenomenon opened up whole new opportunities for community development.

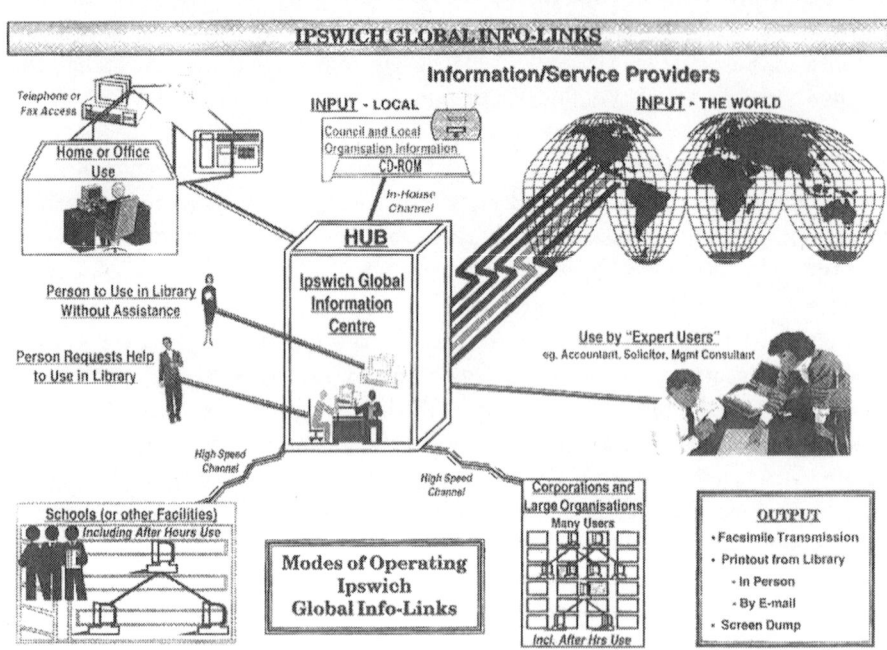

Our 1994 vision of how Global Info Links would work.

In 1994, we defined what we thought an online community was as given below:[13]

> *'... a community with a vision of the future that involves harnessing the power of the Internet and other IT&T technologies in new and innovative ways to empower its residents, institutions, community groups and businesses ...'*

We concluded in our planning phase that an online community would incorporate at least six key characteristics:

- cost-effective access to reliable telecommunications services
- a modern community portal or community intranet
- learning linkages, which foster a continuous learning environment for all citizens
- online community services initiated by local, state, and federal government agencies
- development of an eCommerce marketplace providing new choices and opportunities for local business
- a new higher order of community engagement

When we launched Ipswich as an online community in 1993/94, we were dealing quite explicitly with a program to electronically network a geographic community.

The notion of 'the virtual community' incorporating communities without borders was an exciting concept waiting to be discovered. Online communities of interest, practice, and culture were possible only after the physical connectivity was in place. It is of course worth remembering that communities of interest, practice, and culture at the local level have existed for hundreds of years as community organisations. The network systems we created in the 1990s provided new dimensions for such communities because the new form of connectivity meant communities of interest no longer had or needed geographical borders.

Historically, communities of location have been the most evident and influential. Given the growth in ICTs, communities without geographic borders have grown enormously in sophistication, number, and size over the past ten years, to the point where they are just as, if not more, influential than geographic communities.

With their use of technology, borderless communities tend to be more connected, communicative, and cohesive than many geographic communities. This immense shift has provided a completely new view of how we characterise community behaviour, what

---

[13] Memo from the Ipswich Development Investment Manager to the general manager, Ipswich City Council, 24 June 1994.

constitutes a 'healthy' community, and how we create, empower, develop, transform, and sustain geographic communities. Fifteen years on, given the choice, most people prefer to have the best of both worlds. On one hand, access to the benefits of a first-class community of location, and on the other, access to an exciting array of borderless communities based on interests and practice.

The Global Info-Links Initiative

'... What we accomplished through the IT-led Economic Development Strategy was quite enormous. To see the broader impact on the community of Ipswich was quite phenomenal, the project developed a greater sense of confidence in the community ... we actually had something to be proud of ...'

Peter Gillard, former Global Info-Links Business and Marketing Manager
4 November 2008

The three high profile elements of the Ipswich City Council's Economic Development Strategy 1992-7 (previously outlined[14]) were the new library building (Ipswich Global Information Centre), the new and very original community-owned Internet Service Provider (GIL), and the university campus project. These projects had their origins in two memos from the Ipswich Development Investment Group to the general manager and mayor of the Ipswich City Council on 10 December 1992. All three projects were developed simultaneously during 1993-6. On 4 December 1994, Australia's first ever community owned and operated ISP (GIL) delivered Internet services to the Ipswich community. On 3 February 1995, the Ipswich Global Information Centre (the library) was officially opened, and on 12 December 1996, the University of Queensland publicly announced its commitment to build a campus in Ipswich.

The Ipswich City Council formally adopted its first Economic Development Program which endorsed the principle of 'information technology-led' development in February 1993. The foundation project team to design and build Global Info-Links comprised the corporate manager of development investment (Mal Bryce as Chair), the corporate manager of information systems (Roger Birch), the corporate manager of research and development (Neil McPhillips), the city librarian (Roger Coleman) and the general manager (Jamie Quinn). Margaret Thompson was our invaluable admin support person and Paula Watkins courageously served as my secretary throughout the journey. Political leadership for the project was provided by Councillor Paul Pisasale as Chairman of the Economic Development Committee and the Mayor, Councillor Dave Underwood.

---

[14]   In chapter 2

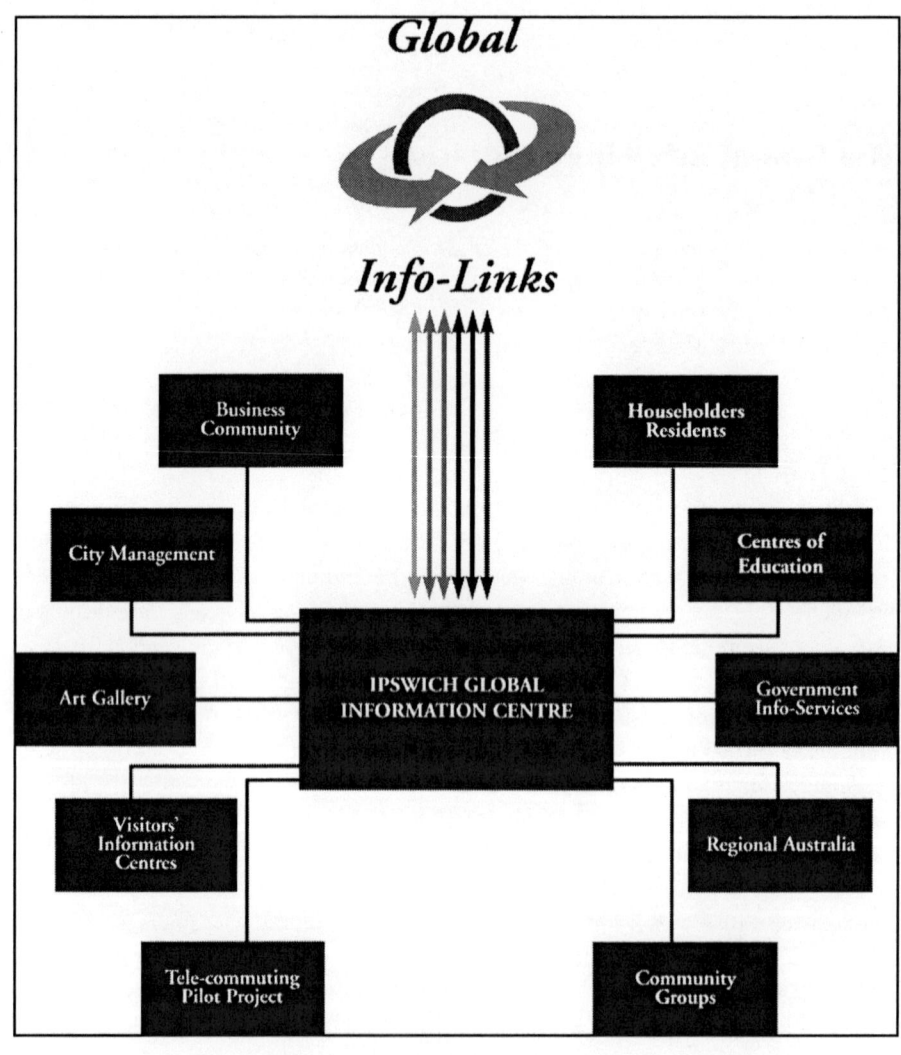

Diagram 1 GIL Schematic

From the very beginning we were focussed on three essential components. A hub, a robust system of networked connections to the world, and a series of what we called local modules. The hub evolved as an ISP located at the heart of a new multi-million dollar library building which we called 'The Ipswich Global Information Centre'. The networked connection became a link to AARNet. At the very early stages of our conceptualising we did not fully comprehend all the relative strengths and weaknesses of Dialogue, AussieNet, ACSNet, and ILA-Net as alternatives to the Internet. We knew we needed access to the best available network, and our friends at the Centre for Information Technology Research firmly recommended the Internet. As a means of growing the customer base we identified ten local modules which became the focus of our activities. Within a very short space of time, we realised the importance of concentrating on the six most important modules namely, householders, centres of education, business, community groups, government, and city management.

Like any major project, the development of the new building and the ISP involved three classic phases—planning and design, construction, and then operation. For almost four calendar years, 1993-6, the project team met every Friday for three to four hours. The resources of four departments of the council—the Ipswich Development Investment Group, the Research and Development Group, the Information Technology Group, the Library—and a significant number of external contractors were drawn upon to make it all happen. The unswerving support at the political level was vital to the success of both projects. Not only did this strategy involve the brand new program of economic development, there were very few people in the world who had ever designed and built an ISP, let alone one of the scale we were contemplating. For a municipality, the Ipswich City Council was breaking new ground. It was inevitable that many key issues would surface from time to time that required the approval of the elected representatives.

The decision to design and build the Global Info-Links hub was based upon the following assumptions:

- The Ipswich City Council was determined that the city should take its place in the Global Information Society.
- Extraordinary levels of investment worldwide were being made in information highways.
- Investment in and access to major information highways of the world would enhance employment prospects at the regional level.
- The telecommunications revolution of the 1980s had fundamentally changed the nature of the following:
  - Management systems
  - Community information systems
  - Basic social and economic interaction

- IT&T-led development would accelerate the normal process of economic development and provide new frontiers and possibilities for the regional economy.
- Ready access to quality information would become increasingly significant in people's lives during the 1990s and beyond.
- Revolutionary breakthroughs in information technology and telecommunications would continue at a dramatic pace throughout the 1990s.
- Global databases were defeating geography.

Our declared mission for the project was 'To make the Ipswich region an information-rich community'.

In lengthy discussions at the time we agreed that basic human creativity would determine what the citizens of Ipswich would do with the information placed at their disposal. Our immediate task was to provide access to that information. Settling on that particular mission statement was an interesting process. From the Global Info-Links records it is interesting to reflect upon some of the other suggestions that were considered as alternative descriptions of our mission. For example, to provide for the citizens of our town better education and training and new business opportunities; to establish a central resource in our town for community information; to promote to the world, our town's core values, priorities, and policies; to enable the citizens of our town to access community services twenty-four hours per day, 365 days per year; to promote our town worldwide as a good place to do business in and to visit and to promote democracy at the local level by facilitating citizen debate on public issues.

The specific objectives of the project were to:

- electronically network the Ipswich community
- ensure universal access to the Internet at reasonable cost
- create jobs through innovation and investment
- improve access to government information
- improve government service delivery

Although the name Global Info-Links became synonymous with the ISP owned and built by the Ipswich City Council, initially as a project title it also incorporated the new library service to be provided to the city.

In early December 1992 the Ipswich City Council received advice from West Moreton Community Health Service (the owners of the building that housed the existing city library), that the library was required to quit the premises within three months. This dramatic news created visions of the city's librarians and their books out on the pavement. Whilst I would like to believe that our compelling logic about the importance of access to the world's great information highways carried the day, in fact it was more likely the sense of urgency to find a new home for the city library that galvanised us into action. Our original plea to the council was 'Let us not rush in and simply build a cardboard cut-out of a traditional library'. The CEO Jamie Quinn accepted the argument that any city builds a new library on average only once per century and that what we should build was a building that would last a century and deliver the services needed well into the next century.

During the planning and construction phases of the Global Info-Links project, there were two specific but closely related components of the concept: the new building which was called the Ipswich Global Information Centre; and Global Info-Links which was the name given to the Internet Service Provider component. The ISP was housed within the new building. From the very earliest times there was a tussle over the decision to name the new building 'The Global Information Centre'. What we were developing was something much greater and more encompassing than a repository for books. The traditionalists within the community were wedded to the notion of a library. (The word Library after all was derived from *librus* meaning books.) It is interesting that after the ISP was corporatised and relocated to another building in the city in 1998, the traditionalists were successful in having the words 'Ipswich City Library' added to the name of the building. This was just one of many cultural adaptations the Ipswich library system had to make in the early to mid-1990s. Opening hours, service functions, staffing rosters, new professional responsibilities, and a host of new electronic systems were other key issues.

Building and Operating an ISP in the early 1990s

'. . . The IT-led Economic Development Strategy worked particularly well to turnaround the internal and external perception of Ipswich . . . Ipswich was invited to be a founding member of the World Technopolis Association. This would never have happened if we had not changed the perception of the City . . .'

Neil McPhillips, former Corporate Manager for R & D and
Economic Development at the Ipswich City Council.
12 September 2008

Fifteen years on, it seems hard to believe that there was no ISP delivering the Internet to the city of Ipswich in 1992 or 1993. In fact there were very few viable ISPs in the world delivering the Internet. Australia's first permanent Internet link to the USA via Melbourne was only established in 1990 by AARNet and was only available for very limited purposes to a restricted number of research based organisations. Given what was available at the time, for our program to work it was necessary to establish our own ISP.

The decision to design, build, and operate our own ISP was not taken lightly. During 1993 and 1994, we researched a vast range of issues including the range of potential services to be offered, user system capabilities, technical architecture, security matters, cost recovery mechanisms, traditional and non-traditional legal issues, infrastructure requirements, and the identification of potential partners. In the decade that followed this ground-breaking work, hundreds of ISP's appeared on the Australian landscape and hundreds of thousands of ISP's appeared worldwide. On the first anniversary of going live (December 1995) the Global Info-Links management team compiled an insightful list of the many practical issues that would influence the future of the project. Those issues identified included the following:

- *The great range in the quality and capacity of existing IT equipment in homes, schools, and businesses.* The variety of gear at the receiver's end created enormous difficulty with expectation management. People who were squeezing the last breath of life out of desktops that were five years old or more did not want to hear that it was perhaps time they upgraded their beloved computer. Many householders still entertained the notion that a computer should last at least as long as the family car or maybe the family beer fridge.

- *Concerns about confidentiality and security and the need for firewalls.* These concerns which don't seem to have diminished over the years were very real. Privacy actually meant something to most people in the 1980s and 1990s. Resolving who could access what information, where, and when, created significant roadblocks for a community that sought to be comprehensively connected. Countless versions of firewalls were produced and sold to organisations about to expose themselves to the hazards of the Internet.

- *The vital importance of local call access and threats by telcos to introduce timed local calls.* With dial-up access to the Internet in the first chapter of online activity the cost of local calls was a critical issue. Had Australian telcos succeeded in their push for timed local calls it would have seriously impeded the development of the Internet revolution.[15] Long after technological breakthroughs brought about the demise of distance as a justification for exorbitant so-called long-distance charges telecommunications carriers worldwide continued to exploit their unknowing customers.

- *The paradigm shift which saw the introduction of advertising on the Internet for the first time.* Of all Net-etiquette issues associated with the early years of access to the Internet, the breaking of the tradition to *never* tolerate commercial advertising was seen by many pioneers and purists as an enormous breach of faith. The evolution of eCommerce and the arrival of commercial ISPs made this inevitable.

- *The impact on local hardware and software retailers of the demand for guidance, support, and after-sales service.* The demands for assistance to get up and running involved a new definition of after-sales service for most computer vendors in the early years of connectivity. It was almost impossible to get non-proprietary brand advice for householders and small businesses interested in connecting to Global Info-Links.

- *The arrival of the debate about inappropriate material on the Internet and the perceived need for the regulation of the new highways.* Following the development of the graphical user-friendly interface for the Internet, it was also inevitable that the debate would emerge about inappropriate material. In our naiveté, the Global Info-Links management team made a credible effort to censor certain lists and news groups. We were quickly confronted by all of the practical and 'in principle' issues associated with censoring the Internet. In

---

[15] The Australian national carrier like so many others around the world was government owned in the early and mid-1990s. The government of the day deemed a policy of timed local calls to be politically unacceptable.

2009, the Chinese government employs 100,000 people in their vain attempt to censor the Net and the Australian government is about to make another rather controversial effort to manage Internet content.

- *The explosive growth in the demand for content development.* The thirst for relevant, interesting, high-quality content was quite extraordinary in the early years of connectivity. Most English language content was very much American. The demand for local content created a wave of both patriotism and opportunity for new small businesses. Graphic designers and web site builders were in short supply. To handle new forms of professional development, universities even began to review their offerings in terms of courses.
- *The central significance of quality control in numerous different aspects of delivering Internet services.* The choking speeds of dial-up narrowband access in the early years, traffic on old copper twisted pairs, competition with voice traffic, and the unreliability of modems all detracted from the reliability of the system.
- *The fundamental need for training and skills development highlighting the vital importance of the help desk.* The number of staff, the hours of operation, and the amount of equipment needed for this essential component of customer service quickly exceeded what had been budgeted for. No one had ever managed a phenomenon such as this before. Whereas we developed the help desk initially with people who were highly technically specialised in networking, many ISPs over the years realised that help desk staff needed people skills before technical skills.
- *The unanticipated speed in the uptake of subscriptions to the service.*
  The uptake of the Internet service was breathtaking. In the first nine months of operation, Global Info-Links sold three thousand five hundred accounts, a figure which exceeded twelve thousand by 1998 and was nudging fifteen thousand by 2000.
- *Constantly emerging new generations of technology to deliver the service.* Perhaps the most daunting task in a technical sense in the 1990s for all ISPs was the dual challenge of keeping up with the explosion in the number and variety of different services expected by subscribers and the lightning pace of technological change sweeping the industry to accommodate the increasingly demanding level of service. This had direct implications for capital budgets and availability of the necessary expertise.

For the vast majority of Australians, connecting to the Internet for the first time in the early 1990s was not simply a novelty but an introduction to a whole new world, one which required new skills and new concepts to be mastered. Of all the leading issues referred to above, the need for training and skills development was paramount. The Global Info-Links management team embarked upon a major program of 'Internet awareness' sessions. Rather than simply building the customer base our imperative was to demonstrate to the citizens of Ipswich how they could exploit and harness the power of the new technology.

The most elementary of all sessions demonstrated how to actually get connected, what was needed to drive a Web browser, how to understand important elements of Internet addresses, learning to successfully download, unpack and configure Internet programs, extending program functionality with plug-ins, add-ons, and upgrades, and how to undertake successful Internet information searches. Within six months of opening, we introduced the concept of the Internet Driver's Licence for the newbies on the information highways.

Special 'Business Awareness' sessions were conducted after the elementary experience and dealt with secure financial transactions and authenticated messaging, authoring techniques to deliver innovative sites, and redefining product, place, price, and promotion on the Web.

Specific Parent Awareness sessions were also run to help families identify the benefits of the Internet for educational purposes and to draw attention to the importance of parent supervision for children using the Net. Until the education module was underway in 1995 most of our customers initially were adults. Therefore, collaborative learning at open public sessions was a key part of the exercise. Adults learn very effectively by listening carefully to the great discoveries, successes, and failures of others.

At a workshop of local users convened in early 1996, the participants outlined a list of the issues that were important to them at that time. The list included things such as:

- how to assess the integrity of information found on the World Wide Web
- developing techniques for effective research
- how to protect children
- understanding online security, firewalls, and viruses
- maintenance, management, and upgrade issues
- buying, downloading, installing, and upgrading software
- intellectual property issues—etiquette, protocols, and legalities
- harnessing and effectively managing the potential of email

At the end of the first decade of the twenty-first century, a similar workshop would probably identify much the same list of issues.

In 1992 and 1993 most Australian capital cities had one or two very embryonic ISPs. All were very much garage ventures. The services delivered by these groups who were essentially hobbyists were notoriously unreliable (frequent dropouts and system crashes) and anything but user-friendly (requiring complicated commands). All delivered a text based service that was available to users via a local dial-up call. Although it was technically feasible, it was not financially practical to connect to the Internet via another city which involved payment for timed calls. (Such was the impact of the old long-distance charging system.) The nearest, almost viable group, to Ipswich was Pegasus based in Byron Bay in NSW, which would have involved Ipswich people meeting long-distance call charges for every minute they spent online. Before the launch of Mosaic in November 1993, none of these embryonic groups could deliver a service that would be appealing to the vast majority of the population. Early connections in Australia to ACSNet (which was not the Internet) and the Internet were relevant only for technically savvy individuals amounting to no more than 1-2 percent of the population. Perhaps the major drawback to these early network connections was the presentation of material in dull and boring green text on a black screen.

The first demonstration of the Internet in Ipswich arranged by the IDI group at the Ipswich City Council occurred on 12 January 1993 in the council chambers to an audience of curious and somewhat sceptical city Aldermen and senior staff.

That demonstration was presented by Rob Cook and his team from the Centre for Information Technology Research at the University of Queensland. It is a miracle to this day that the temporary connection to the university (approximately 45 kilometres away) did not drop out during the demonstration. In his recollection of that moment, Rob Cook stated the following:

> '... my recollections are all about the stupidity (in 1993) of trying to put on
> a live demonstration on a fragile network all that distance from the hub ...
> I can remember sitting there petrified that it would breakdown during the
> demonstration ...'[16]

The information presented that day in 1993 was projected onto a large black screen in classic boring green text. For the record, software called Gopher was used to locate databases such as Archie, Veronica, and Jughead, a far cry from the age of Google. The council was sufficiently impressed and soon after gave us approval to develop and implement the Ipswich Information Links Initiative. Before the end of 1993 we had added the word 'Global' to the title.

During the debrief following the demonstration, I can recall commenting to Rob Cook that as interesting as the Internet looked it was dead in the water as far as the general community was concerned without a graphical user-friendly interface. We reached agreement that day that if we were given approval to proceed with the project we would go out to tender in the marketplace and find a software company to develop an attractive graphical user-friendly interface. We did in fact include a significant allocation in our original budget for this task. CiTR had by the end of the year drawn up the specs for this

---

[16]   Interview with Rob Cook, 12 September 2008, formerly CEO of Centre for Information Technology Research, University of Queensland.

tender. At the eleventh hour as we were about to put the contract out to tender, I received a phone call from Richard Naylor, a friend and fellow Internet pioneer in Wellington, New Zealand, informing us of the birth and release of Mosaic in Switzerland. Mosaic is the often forgotten precursor to Netscape and Internet Explorer. This was a wonderful timely breakthrough that saved us a considerable sum of money. I have often reminded Richard that that phone call was one of the more important and timely calls I have ever received. It was in fact a rather audacious step we had contemplated that would have led the whole world to our door had we proceeded and been successful before Mosaic.

Once the decision in principle to build our own ISP was taken we obviously needed technical advice on how to do just that in the most cost-effective manner. The Ipswich City Council entered into a Memorandum of Understanding with CiTR in early 1993, and our project team enjoyed a highly creative and successful relationship with them through to completion of the project in December 1994. The design for a vehicle (subsequently called an ISP) to provide reliable, user-friendly access to the Internet was delivered to us in the form of a Technical Framework Study by CiTR. Our in-house IT specialists including Dave Sutton, Chris Nilon, Rudolph Mueller, and Andrew Osborne had the job of building it. Geoff Huston at AARNet in Canberra proved to be one of our most valuable external allies. Geoff worked as one of a very small team to build the Internet in Australia from its very inception. He not only gave us a sympathetic hearing as the first Australian community to ask for connection to the Internet, he actually visited Ipswich on several occasions to speak at our awareness sessions. It was very handy in 1994 and early 1995 to have a guru from the national capital visit our city and explain to councillors and ratepayers alike that the journey we were embarking upon was both timely and achievable. Other external commercial organisations to play a creative role in casting the shape of the venture in those early stages of implementation included Data 3, Datamaster, JTech, Interactive Presentations, and Arthur Advertising.

Building an ISP as an information hub for the community was very much about the telecommunications part of IT&T. Only a few months into the planning process for Global Info-Links it occurred to us that we did not really know a great deal about the telecommunications infrastructure within Ipswich or for that matter the infrastructure that connected Ipswich to the world. Our project team agreed that we faced a dilemma if we built the equivalent of an autobahn in parts of Ipswich and then faced debilitating bottlenecks in our endeavours to get out to the world.

We decided in our naivety to approach Telecom which was morphing into Telstra at the time and asked them some basic questions about the existing infrastructure. Questions such as, how many switching stations there were in the city, which ones were analogue and which were digital, how old the infrastructure was, what Telstra's plans were for upgrade, how full the pipes were, how much copper versus fibre cable there was in the infrastructure mix, and of course, what sort of speeds could be guaranteed. For many of us this was our first ever conversation about bandwidth. We had had the temerity to ask, and we were about to be very surprised by Telstra's response. We very soon discovered that we were the first community in Australian history to ask our great government-owned telecommunications monopoly for this information. They had never been asked for this information before and had no intention of providing it. We on the other hand knew where all the roads, footpaths, power lines, water, and sewerage lines in the city were and in order to develop a truly connected community needed to know a great deal more about the telecommunications infrastructure. Months passed and we heard nothing.

Finally, we arranged to meet Frank Blunt, the CEO of Telecom/Telstra in Brisbane, only to be told that the information we sought had important security implications and was available on a need-to-know basis only. Either we did not need to know or we were potential security risks. We were appalled at this turn of events. Our immediate instincts were to insist upon a meeting with the Federal Minister for Telecommunication, Michael Lee, MHR, in Canberra as soon as possible. That meeting was held within three weeks and the Minister was sympathetic to our cause. Eventually, he had to actually direct Telecom to provide us with the information we sought. When it arrived, it amounted to the bare minimum. The process had been akin to drawing wisdom teeth. Our working relationships with Telecom was somewhat strained for the rest of 1993.

Since that experience numerous other local governments in Australia have sought and received similar information from the national carrier, information that amounts to a telecommunications mud map of their town. Since 1997 and the introduction of an increasing number of private Telcos, it has become standard procedure to undertake an audit of the telecommunications infrastructure for communities embarking on serious digital strategies. Telecom gained their revenge in early 1994 when we asked for five hundred lines coming into the new building. They begrudgingly gave us two hundred lines, and we had to beg for more in 1995 as the volume of traffic and the number of subscribers expanded beyond everyone's wildest expectations.

The Global Info Links logo designed by
Linwood Rae.
An image that quickly spread
around the world in 1994/5

The earliest available screen grab of the
Global Info Links home page 1997.

Courtesy of the "Way Back Then" website

The engine room of one of the
world's largest ISPs in 1994. In the
background stands the first of many
"Totem Poles" of 14.4 Kps modems.

Photo: Courtesy of Lyle Radford

Hon Barry Jones (former Australian Minister
for Science and Technology) officiating
at the Opening of the Ipswich Global
Information Centre February 3rd 1995

Photo: Courtesy of Queensland Times.

Hon Barry Jones and former Mayor
of Ipswich Dave Underwood

Photo: Courtesy of Queensland Times.

Opening Day for the Ipswich Global
Information Centre February 3rd 1995.

Photo: Courtesy of Queensland Times.

The Ipswich Global Information Centre. A
symbol of renewal for the City of Ipswich

Photo: Courtesy of Lyle Radford

Part 3

Outcomes

• Connecting the Community
• A New World-Class Library and Information Service
• Schools Online (the Education Module)
• SeniorNet
• Businesses Online (eCommerce and the Business Module)
• Local, State, and Federal Government Services Online
• A University Campus for Ipswich: The Twin Project

Connecting the Community

'. . . As a community strategy to bring technology into this city, Global Info-Links served its purpose tenfold . . . it was facilitating the interests of so many different people across the board . . .'

Darryl Cross, former Global Info-Links Development Manager
10 September 2008

The power and functionality of computers increased exponentially during the 1980s. In terms of networking, various systems had been developed that would enable machines to talk to machines in terms of transferring data. The key that was missing by the end of the 1980s was the means to cheaply and reliably enable humans to interact in the process.

My own introduction to the world of the new information highways and the significance of the convergence of computing and telecommunications had occurred in 1989-90 during my work with the UN in Geneva. I outlined the original concept for a new generation Ipswich Information Service with my friend and colleague, Neil McPhillips, in early December 1992. He and I fondly recall that it was after work at the Ipswich RSL Club. We fundamentally agree that many great and some not-so-great innovations have been born over a few beers with evidence of genius like insights to be found the next day on the back of a drink coaster. Diagram 2 outlines the vision. A copy of this sketch in the author's best handwriting (after a couple of drinks) is the first item in the massive Ipswich City Council filing system that records the Global Info-Links journey. Diagram 3 is the first official schematic representation of the concept.

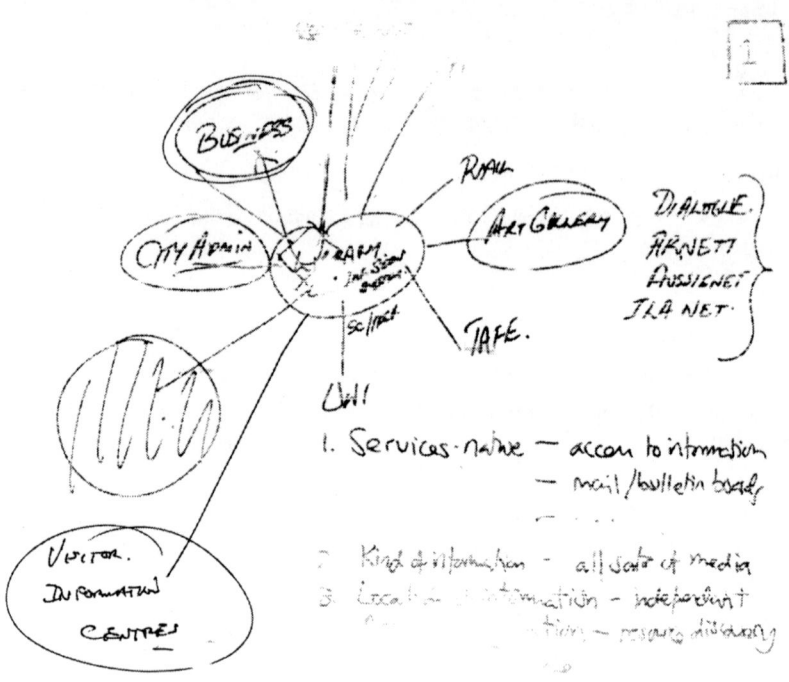

Diagram 2: The original unsophisticated outline of the vision Dec 1992

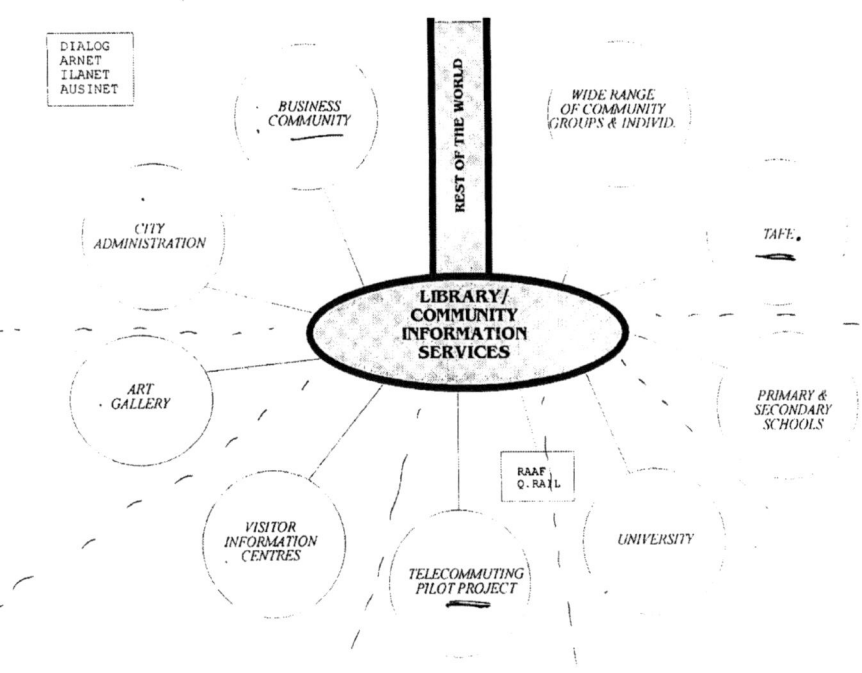

DIALOG
ARNET
ILANET
AUSINET

BUSINESS
COMMUNITY

REST OF THE WORLD

WIDE RANGE
OF COMMUNITY
GROUPS & INDIVID.

CITY
ADMINISTRATION

TAFE.

LIBRARY/
COMMUNITY
INFORMATION
SERVICES

ART
GALLERY

PRIMARY &
SECONDARY
SCHOOLS

RAAF
Q.RAIL

VISITOR
INFORMATION
CENTRES

UNIVERSITY

TELECOMMUTING
PILOT PROJECT

Diagram 3 Version 2 of GIL Schematic

General connectivity between families, community organisations, and government agencies had improved remarkably during the 1970s and 1980s. In Ipswich in the early 1970s approximately 45 percent of homes had landline connections to telephones. By the early 1990s that figure was 97 percent. Mobile phones began to arrive in the mid-1980s, but by 1992 very few people owned or operated one in Ipswich. They were still bulky, heavy, and expensive to run. Needless to say SMS messaging was not yet a twinkle in the eye of its creator. Based on a survey done by the GIL project team in 1993/4 less than 40 percent of homes in Ipswich had a PC although approximately 50 percent of homes with children under the roof had one. The vast majority of those computers were 386 and 486 machines and very early versions of Apple Mac. Sixty-five percent of businesses owned and operated a PC. Laptop computers were arriving, but for most people and small businesses they were prohibitively expensive. It is reasonable to assume that 100 percent of homes and businesses were connected to electricity.

There is an old adage in the IT industry that until computers (PCs) could talk to each other there was no real reason for the bulk of the population to own one. Here in lies the essential contribution of the Internet. The telephone in everyone's home by 1993/4 provided voice contact for subscribers. The TCP and IP protocols refined during the 1980s meant that data could now be transmitted on the lines designed for voice traffic.

The primary objective of the Global Info-Links project was to take advantage of this breakthrough in technology. We were determined to make Ipswich an information-rich community by connecting the city to the great databases of the world and by greatly enhancing connectivity within the city between households and community organisations. In a rapidly emerging information economy we had reached the conclusion that access to top quality information at the moment you needed it was vital to local economic and community development.

Our plans for the roll-out of Global Info-Links involved three stages.

Stage One: Comprised the construction of the Internet hub and the provision of basic online connectivity for all Ipswich households and community organisations.

Stage Two: Was a commitment to build what we called the business module and thereby provide access to the global electronic market. We ambitiously set ourselves two years to achieve this 1995/6

Stage Three: Involved a rather audacious plan to hard-wire the CBD of the city of Ipswich with seriously fast bandwidth.

At the outset of our project to take the services offered by the Internet to the people of Ipswich, we understood that the critical limitation confronting us was the inadequacy of the painfully slow dial-up narrowband access to the Internet. In 1995, in Wollongong and Canberra, national pilot projects to be funded by the Federal government for the roll-out of broadband infrastructure had been mooted. With great gusto, we had the temerity to suggest that Ipswich should become a third pilot project based on the ground-breaking work of Global Info-Links. We estimated that a pilot project involving 500-1,000 broadband connections within the Ipswich CBD emanating from the Ipswich Global Information Centre would cost somewhere in the vicinity of $2.5-$3 million. The pilot would be preceded by a feasibility study costing $100,000. The Ipswich City Council applied to the Federal Department of Housing and Regional Development for this funding. In their wisdom the Federal government rejected our request for inclusion in their national pilot program and the feasibility study.

Fifteen to twenty years later, at much greater cost, the National Broadband Network will eventually deliver this dream.

Such was the explosive growth in the demand for data after the popularisation of the Internet that by 1998 the volume of data traffic surpassed the volume of voice traffic in Australia for the first time. Using a copper wire based system designed for voice traffic as the means of transferring a rapidly increasing volume of data created many problems. The most memorable of these was (and still is to some extent) the matter of speed. People using email increased the complexity of attachments to their messages, and second, third, and fourth generation web sites began to feature bandwidth-hungry bells and whistles. The world's most famous acronym WWW came to mean the great World Wide Wait. Congestion rapidly became a major problem for the telecommunications infrastructure. Most early ISPs had to operate a time limit for connections, after which subscribers were simply dropped off and had to take their chances by dialling in again. When Global Info-Links opened for business in 1994, the first bank of modems operated at 9.6 Kbps. During the next six years, modem speeds increased progressively to 14.4, 28.8, 33.3, 56, and finally, 128 Kbps. There was always great excitement associated with the release of each new generation of 'high-speed' modem. Throughout most of the 1990s, despite the gradually increased modem speeds Telstra only ever guaranteed a speed from its end of 9.6 Kbps. In households and businesses alike there was ever present the matter of conflict of use. Whilst the standard landline was being used for Internet purposes (data transfer) it could not be used for voice purposes. In the early years this led many subscribers to install a second landline. These fundamental limitations persisted until the arrival of the first generation of broadband connections (speeds in excess of 200 Kbps) after 1998. If the early arrivals amongst Global Info-Links customers were frustrated by the slow connection speeds, that frustration paled into insignificance compared with the frustration experienced by the managers of the system.

Timed calls related to distance and speeds for data transfer dictated by bandwidth became the essential preoccupations for almost a decade for those of us who were committed to delivering the economic and social benefits of the ICT revolution.

Global Info-Links managers were painfully aware that a few hundred metres from our ISP in Ipswich there existed a fibre cable backbone, capable of breathtaking speeds that was owned by Queensland Rail. The nine-core cable with seven unused cores (dark fibre) ran all the way to Brisbane. Particular provisions of the Australian government's Telecommunications Act at the time meant that we were not permitted to access that cable. Queensland Rail was prohibited from granting access to any third parties.

With this very modest level of computer penetration in the community and what now seems like a 'dark age' form of networking, we approached the moment when we would go live with great excitement. The building was completed, the ISP was finished, and all we needed were customers. In actual anticipation of that moment, we decided that we would scour the community to identify one hundred foundation customers. We called them our Project Champions. In return for signing up, they were offered six months free access. When the building was officially opened by the former mayor, Dave Underwood, and former Federal Minister for Technology, Barry Jones, MHR, on 3 February 1995, GIL already had its first five hundred customers. Two years later the subscriber family had reached 4,500. By August 1998, it had passed 10,000 and peaked at just over 15,000 in 2001 when GIL became part of the new community telecommunications company, iTEL.

In the words of Paul Casos, CEO of South East Queensland Community Telco,[17]

> '. . . When Bendigo Bank came to Queensland, they brought with them a model for a community-owned telecommunications company which they had trialled in Bendigo Victoria. They advised the Ipswich City Council that they were establishing the Queensland headquarters of the bank in Ipswich and that they were also intending to establish a community-owned telecommunications company in Ipswich. Agreement was reached between the bank and Ipswich City Council to jointly establish an unlisted public company called iTEL, short for Ipswich Telecommunications, which would acquire the Internet company from the Ipswich City Council . . . If it wasn't for the fact that Global Info-Links was established in this city (and it has grown into iTEL) there is no way that telecommunication services would be as competitive as they are in this town today . . .'

The Bendigo Bank subsequently established a parent organisation called Community Telco Australia. Under that umbrella, successful community telcos operate in the Sunshine Coast, Newcastle, Dubbo, Bathurst, Orange, Geelong, Ballarat, Launceston, and Hobart in addition to Ipswich and Bendigo.

---

[17]   Interview with Paul Casos, 5 November 2008.

One of the most frequently asked questions over many years has been, 'What did it cost and how was it financed?' The answer is fairly crisp. The Ipswich Global Information Centre building including fit out cost approximately $12.5 million and the initial cost of the ISP was $800,000. The Ipswich City Council funded $11 million. Two million dollars was received from the Queensland State Government and a grand total of $300,000 was received from the federal government. Most importantly the funding from the Ipswich City Council was from its balance sheet. The city under the firm guidance of its CEO, Jamie Quinn, and Finance Committee Chairman, Councillor Paul Tully, had some years before embarked upon a determined program to be debt free by 2000 and was in excellent financial shape.

Budget discussions in 1993, 1994, and 1995 were most interesting occasions as money was actually shaved from the Works Department for this new groundbreaking project. In some senses it became a choice between information highways and traditional blacktop highways. I hasten to add that not all the Ipswich City Council's funding for this project was found at the expense of the Works Department. Given the choice not many local governments in the world in the early 1990s would have come down on the side of the information highways. The $2 million from the Queensland Government did not arrive without a public policy struggle. In traditional terms, Ipswich city was building a new library and was entitled to a $2 million grant towards the cost of fit out, especially for books. It took us nine months to convince the state government that we were all entering a new age and that at least part of the $2 million grant could and should be spent on ICT equipment. Our efforts in this respect made a humble contribution to Queensland public policy. The $300,000 from the federal government was so inconsequential that no one can quite remember which particular program it came from.

For those with a technical bent the ISP hub amounted to a break with tradition. Unlike normal bulletin board services emerging in the early 1990s, GIL was not set up on a network of PCs. The new Ipswich phenomenon boasted a Hewlett Packard Precision Architecture-Reduced Instruction Set Computing E25. It also used a dedicated UNIX server as opposed to an Intel-based computer. The system had what was accepted at the time as a huge 128 megabytes of memory and fifteen gigabytes storage capacity, both capable of ready expansion. In terms of speed of access the system could cope with any speed up to 14,400 baud. Global Info-Links started life with thirty-two modems which grew to 400 modems by 1997. The system was designed to be able to grow to take up to 1,000 simultaneous connections. GIL's initial ISDN link to the Internet was 64 K.

Subscribers to Global Info-Links purchased blocks of time which could be used on a varied and individual basis. Blocks of time were sold in monthly, quarterly, and annual lots. If customers had not used up their allocated time by a particular expiry date, they were able to roll over any unused hours into their next subscription. The charges of

1995 make interesting reading. On a monthly basis forty hours cost $56. On a quarterly basis, 130 hours cost $162.50, and on an annual basis 520 hours cost $520.00. This meant a range from $1 per hour to $1.40 per hour. At that time Pegasus based in Byron Bay was charging $6.56 per hour, Oz email in Sydney, $5-$10 per hour, and Microsoft Network, $5 per hour. Global Info-Links consciously set a scale of fees which it was felt Ipswich ratepayers could afford to pay. Universal access at reasonable cost was one of GIL's basic objectives.

Initially, the services provided in return for these charges were access to email, newsgroups, Web browsing, Gopher browsing, Telnet, and FTP. In addition, subscribers were offered the ability to create their own home page.

Based on information provided by the GIL management team in 1998, by August of that year, Global Info-Links

- had over 10,000 subscribers
- had approximately 4,000 business clients
- hosted over 350 business web sites
- offered twenty-five Internet services to clients
- had links to all 121 schools in the Ipswich Region
- was handling 800 calls per week to the help desk
- boasted 50,000 impressions per week on its web site
- had an estimated revenue for 1997/98 of a $2 million

At that time there were also more than 3,000 personal visits per week to the Ipswich Global Information Centre, and Global Info-Links was operating as a commercial business unit within the Ipswich City Council, making a modest profit and providing a return on investment to the city council.

From its inception in December 1994 to its incorporation into iTEL in 2001, Global Info-Links effectively passed through four phases. Initially it was developed and managed as a division of the IDI Group and the economic program of the Ipswich City Council. Between 1998 and 2000 it was run as a commercial business unit within the Ipswich City Council. In the same period the Ipswich city Waste Management System and Water Supply System were also restructured as commercial business units of the Ipswich City Council under the influence of the National Competition Policy. In 2000, Global Info-Links Pty Ltd was established (with the Ipswich City Council as the sole shareholder) at a time when most Australian ISPs were morphing into telecommunications companies.

Confronted with the prospects of running a telecommunications company in a highly complex market place, the Ipswich City Council reached an agreement with the

Bank of Bendigo to merge Global Info-Links with the new community telco, iTEL, in 2001. Global Info-Links as an entity became the Internet component of iTEL. iTEL subsequently changed its name to the South East Queensland Community Telecommunications Company in 2008.

It's Worth Remembering That . . .

In 1992, when we embarked upon our rather audacious journey,
Ipswich, Australia, and the world were very different places.

- PCs were not widespread. Dumb terminals featuring black screens and green characters were in most large organisations.
- Laptop computers were only just arriving.
- Very few people had ever heard the word *Internet*.
- No one had an email address on their business card.
- The word broadband was not in general usage.
- Mobile phones which were as heavy and as large as a house brick and very expensive had been around for a few years.
- The first SMS was years away from being sent.
- The world's first web server was built in 1991 and the world's first web pages were published in 1992.
- URLs were unknown.
- No Australian businesses, government agencies, or communities had web sites.
- Google was not yet a dream for Larry Page and Sergey Brin (the founders).

A New World-Class Library and Information Service

'. . . Global Info-Links was established before I arrived in Ipswich. When I observed GIL from afar, I was struck by the fact that the connection between the library and information technology had been established . . . previously libraries were not part of information technology thinking . . .'

Narelle Rhodes, Ipswich City Library Services Manager since 2000
5 November 2008

If we were correct to assume in the early 1990s that the post-industrial economy would evolve as the information economy it made sense to develop a fully integrated information service for the Ipswich community. With the passage of time it became clear that the new integrated information service became a tool for community and social development every bit as much as economic development.

Fifteen years into the first one hundred years of its life, the Ipswich Global Information Centre has been magnificently maintained and is a first-class asset to the city. The building constitutes a world-class contemporary facility, housing some very special teams of people and delivering a fully integrated information service to the citizens of Ipswich. During the 1990s the $800,000 ISP (Global Info-Links) attracted the lion's share of publicity to the project because the Internet was a spectacularly new and world-changing technology. Today, hundreds of ISPs operate in Australia, and Global Info-Links has become an integral part of The South East Queensland Telecommunications Company, in which the Ipswich City Council is a shareholder.

The $12.5 million Ipswich Global Information Centre building has become an iconic example of a highly successful contemporary integrated information service. At the outset it was designed to be so much more than a repository for books. With the exception of the ISP, the building today houses basically the same teams of people (economic development, information systems, and librarians) who were located there on opening day (3 February 1995). Approximately one hundred and thirty people work in the building today and include library staff (58), Ipswich City

Council Information Systems branch (31), Ipswich City Council Marketing branch (20), Economic and Community Development branch (10), the Events branch (4), and the Media branch (4). The building incorporates a coffee shop, an auditorium, a state-of-the-art presentation room and numerous meeting and study rooms, which all serve to broaden the concept of a serious community hub for an information service-cum-learning centre.

Library-based information services have existed for generations wherever there have been libraries. Librarians in a professional capacity had been accessing databases in the 1980s and an increasing proportion of their customers had begun accessing libraries via the telephone with requests for information. Our decision to add the Internet service to what was on offer at the Ipswich City Library in 1994 was integrating the new online world with the traditional off line sources of information. From 1994 in Ipswich, librarians had access to the Internet to assist them in providing a first rate information service to their customers.

In the words of Cathy Watson, a senior librarian, who has probably had the longest continuous association with Global Info-Links,[18]

> '. . . For the first time it was us acting as facilitators instead of gatekeepers to information . . . it was a challenging role because the technology was changing so fast . . .'

The new library itself also contained fourteen multimedia public access terminals where for a very modest charge, members of the public themselves could gain access to the ocean of information on the Internet. Fully fledged video conferencing facilities together with technical support were also available to library users. More importantly the city council's very own ISP situated in the library was designed to provide Internet services to households, schools, community organisations, and local businesses. When we were planning this service in 1993, there was no ISP in Australia that was sufficiently robust to be able to guarantee local call access to the Internet for the residents of Ipswich.

When we established the Ipswich Global Information Centre as Australia's first eLibrary, we were frequently asked what 'electronic library' meant. Our 1995 explanation was the following:[19]

---

[18]   Interview with Cathy Watson, 11 September 2008.
[19]   Global Info-Links, published by the Ipswich City Council, 1995.

A concept made possible by the inter-relationship and interactivity of:

- traditional 'book' library service managed through Dynix Horizon Software which also provides members with user-friendly online computer access to the library catalogue
- an ISP (Global Info-Links) providing Internet access to the community
- public access computers providing Internet, multimedia, and CD ROM services
- the hub of Australia's fastest high-speed city council local area network
- a modern video conference system
- the home of the most advanced geographic information system in Australia— the first to fully harness digital orthophotography
- satellite reception
- a first-class electronic presentation room

In the sense that GIL (now incorporated into the SEQ Community Telco) is in 2009 one of hundreds of ISPs in Australia, the pioneering efforts of the Ipswich library staff during the decade that followed 1995 have been incorporated into library information services all over Australia. These efforts have included the role of the interactive library web service, the introduction of the concept of the eCollection, the online readers list, remote access to the library catalogue, the provision of public access machines (to the Internet), swipe card technology for public access machines, the ability to download audio books, and the introduction of SMS messaging to library clients.

New technology has become an important part but certainly, only a part, of a truly effective library information service as are the buildings themselves which house the services. In the words of Narelle Rhodes who has been Ipswich Library Manager since 2000,[20]

> '. . . Overall there is recognition that it is not enough to build great library buildings. What makes the difference is what happens when the library engages strategically in the community . . . there is certainly increasing emphasis on the development of libraries as community hubs that foster social cohesion and engagement and that promote learning in the community. Key mechanisms are partnerships and strategic outreach and programming . . .'

Under the leadership of Narelle Rhodes, the Ipswich Library has played a key role in fostering lifelong learning especially in partnership with a wide range of educational institutions and learning providers.

---

[20]   Ipswich Library and Information Service: 'Coping with Growth', Paper published for the Ipswich City Council, November 2008.

The Ipswich Library Info Coach program involves interaction with schools to demonstrate the importance of information literacy skills. The Your Tutor interactive online service for students between Grades 4-12 provides direct assistance to primary and secondary students. The city's mobile library service has a satellite connection to facilitate online interactivity irrespective of location.

Special engagement sessions are available to teachers to demonstrate the learning potential of blogs, wickies, and numerous other aspects of social networking. For many years, the Ipswich Library has employed a training coordinator to provide training to the community and to the library staff to develop and maintain their skill levels in a world of rapidly changing technology.

Not unlike the programs of SeniorNet, the Ipswich Global Information Centre has played a lead pioneering role in Australia since 1995 in delivering its IT training opportunities, where customers can:

- explore the basics of the Internet visiting useful and informative sites
- learn the fundamentals of word processing
- create, edit, print, and save basic documents
- download image and sound files
- sign up for a live email account and learn how to manage an email system
- send photo and text attachments with emails
- explore online sites where it is possible to edit, enhance, and share digital photos
- create individual digital scrapbooks via PowerPoint
- explore options for the safe use of the Internet

Narelle Rhodes sums up this field of activity as,[21]

> '. . . Building a learning city one person at a time . . . it's about connecting people with information, educating them, providing them with information literacy skills and being there when they need help . . .'

There seems little doubt that libraries worldwide have undergone significant change since the introduction and popularisation of the Internet in 1994/95. The future will clearly involve these very proud institutions in becoming more flexible as centres for community development. A role that will require new resources to break down isolation, engage youth, focus on areas of special need and foster stronger social cohesion.

---

[21]   Interview with Narelle Rhodes, 5 November 2008.

Schools Online (the Education Module)

'... When the Ipswich City Council gave every Ipswich school a modem (December 1994) I thought that was one of the most revolutionary things that had ever happened in the world ... in early 1995 when I asked the P&C for more computers for the school I told them we were now part of a project that was going to revolutionise the world ...'

Poppy Masselos: Head Star Education Editor 'The Courier Mail'
Brisbane; former teacher at St Mary's School Ipswich
11 September 2008

The education module of Global Info-Links was the first module that virtually exploded into action. The energy for the beginnings of what has amounted to an education revolution was to be found in two Ipswich Primary Schools, namely Bundamba Primary School and St Mary's Primary School. Lindy McKeown at Bundamba and Poppy Masselos at St Mary's were both human dynamos and visionaries. In both cases they were individual teachers within their respective schools who recognised in 1994 that the world was about to change in a major way. Like most schools in Australia at that time the staff generally were digitally challenged, telephone lines (for connectivity) were not available to teachers in classrooms, and the quality of computing equipment was questionable. To quote Poppy Masselos, most Australian schools in the early 1990s could possibly have boasted of '... a couple of computers in a couple of classrooms ...'[22]

The number of homes in Ipswich which had a computer was always a matter of real concern to us. We were never exactly sure because it had not yet occurred to the Australian Bureau of Statistics that they should ask this leading question at census time. As a very crude measure we asked a number of teachers to conduct straw poll surveys in classrooms. In 1995 our best estimate was that approximately 38 percent of Ipswich homes with school-aged children under the roof had a computer of some description and 5 percent had more than one. For the city as a whole, this percentage would have been lower. During the course of the straw poll exercise, one teacher reported that in

---

[22]   Interview with Poppy Masselos, 11 September 2008

a particular classroom of eight-year-olds, 35 percent of students claimed to have a computer at home, 4 percent claimed to have two computers, and a very enthusiastic student said, '. . . Sir, we have ten computers at our house, but Dad keeps eight of them in the ceiling . . .'. We never enquired what business Dad was in.

Our experience in the education world further illustrated the argument that information technology was of limited relevance to the majority of people until computers could talk to each other.

Within days of going live on 8 December 1994, the Ipswich City Council made an important gesture that effectively kick-started the use of the Internet in Australian primary and secondary schools. As with Lindy McKeown at Bundamba Primary School and Poppy Masselos at St Mary's, there were probably other individual teachers in various parts of the country researching and evaluating the potential of the Internet for educational purposes during 1993 and 1994. As a general tool for use in education, the Internet would only be of real value once the graphical user-friendly interface (Mosaic) was available; prior to that it was destined to be a curio of relevance to very few. There were two key parts to the gesture by the Ipswich City Council. Firstly, the council donated a modem to each of the 121 schools in the Ipswich Region,[23] and secondly, each school was granted 800 hours of free access. We were keen for all our local schools to play and discover. Approximately, half the schools took up the offer before the long Christmas break. The reaction, given below, of Poppy Masselos reflected her infectious enthusiasm:

> '. . . I cancelled a holiday trip to America that Christmas and spent six weeks online. It was like the whole world being brought to my living room, and I basically stayed in my pyjamas for my holidays . . .'[24]

The GIL Management team early in 1995 established an Education Advisory Group, comprising of ten interested local teachers. With their assistance we then embarked upon a program of Internet Awareness sessions where the potential of the new network was regularly demonstrated and as time went by where classic case studies were presented. The first and most celebrated case study was presented to our Education Advisory Group soon after school resumed from summer holidays in February 1995 by a fifteen-year-old boy. Rowan McCarthy had a passionate interest in the sinking of the Titanic and constructed what would probably have been Australia's first and potentially the world's first web site to be built by a secondary school student. Under

---

[23] The Ipswich Region comprised Ipswich City Council plus the four neighboring rural local governments.

[24] Interview with Poppy Masselos, 11 September 2008

Lindy McKeown's leadership Bundamba Primary was in all probability the first school in Australia to have a web site.

With pressure from Poppy Masselos, the Ipswich daily newspaper, *The Queensland Times,* launched a new column to spread the word. Called CYBER POP, for almost four years the column provided a running commentary to the people of Ipswich on fascinating web sites, new applications, and new search engines. This column was also syndicated to the *Adelaide Advertiser and the Hobart Mercury.* Wearing her hat as teacher/innovator, Poppy Masselos also launched OZ KIDZ INTERNAUT CYBER CENTRE which quickly became a publishing place for children's art and writing.

Inevitably, the implications for the Queensland School system of widespread access to the Internet would shift to the state government. The Ipswich Education Advisory Group was during its existence conscientious in its identification of the key issues and forces that would ultimately have a major impact on education. A representative sample of those key issues included recognition that:

- the learning process, the basic education environment, and virtually all training institutions would undergo some profound changes
- electronically networked information would pose serious challenges to traditional repositories of books and even CDs
- increasing demands for high-capacity bandwidth would test the telecommunications infrastructure available to all centres of learning
- professional development for an army of educators trained before the digital era would become vital to our competitiveness
- the need for technical support and back up would become an issue of real concern to educators
- communications between schools and parents would alter quite radically
- all learning environments would incorporate the use of interactive CD ROMS and the Internet
- the demand for keyboarding skills would become ubiquitous
- school systems would have to navigate their way through a maze of issues associated with acceptable and inappropriate material
- increased access to IT&T would greatly expand options for extracurricular activities
- increased time devoted to online activities would require extra effort aimed at fitness and physical recreation

There were identifiable benefits for students, teachers, and parents. Students had access to a greater range of information, opportunities were emerging for the online classroom, and there were more flexible options available in education. Teachers had more effective access to best practise examples in education and training, could enjoy a wider professional network, and new in-service education and training opportunities. Parents could benefit from new worlds of information, new forms of involvement in their children's education, and new opportunities for their own lifelong education.

At the post secondary level of education, especially TAFE, it became clear that a global education market open twenty-four hours would emerge, that virtual classrooms with networked remote sites would challenge 'chalk and talk' and that electronic publications were exploding in number.

SeniorNet

'. . . *Something we have actually all learned over this last fifteen to twenty years is that there is no substitute for human to human contact . . . people of this modern age need both online and direct human contact . . .*'

Gordon Timbs, President of Ipswich SeniorNet.
5 November 2008

In the context of the original model for Global Info-Links we intended to initially develop six modules which were to be connected to the Internet hub. For each module, we developed a program and a set of priorities.

Very early into the life of Global Info-Links, it became clear that ideas for additional modules were almost unlimited. We could very easily have increased the number of modules to twenty or more. Rather than partially or imperfectly develop a large number of modules, we chose to carefully develop the original six . . . with one exception. That exception was SeniorNet. We felt at the time that there was sound logic to justify such an initiative.

Seniors represented an increasingly significant percentage of the population and had a wealth of information and experience to share with younger generations. Modern businesses, education institutions, and governments were increasingly conducting their operations using computing technology, the skills base for which was not available to retirees and seniors in general. Seniors interested in an independent and productive lifestyle were increasingly aware of this opportunity gap.

Whilst their children and grandchildren had embraced computing for communications, education, and recreation purposes, many seniors were reluctant and lacked the opportunities to come to grips with the new technology. This reality had the potential to widen the generation gap.

I outlined the concept of a SeniorNet originally to Jamie Quinn (CEO), and in his response he wasted few words. His answer was simply 'Hilda des Arts'. If we were to do it, we needed someone to drive it, and Dr Hilda des Arts was the obvious choice.

A feature writer for the *Sunday Mail* on the 12 February 1995 described Hilda in the following terms:[25]

> '. . . *An eighty-year-old grandmother who has retired to the future whose living room in her neat brick bungalow in Ipswich looks like the bridge of Starship Enterprise. An industrial strength computer, a high speed modem, an inkjet printer and a facsimile machine dominate her living room. There is not enough space for the photocopier so it's been shoehorned into her bedroom. She purchased her first personal computer at seventy years of age and taught herself to use it from a tutorial disk. Ten years later she is launching a mission to take senior citizens into cyberspace . . .*'

When asking Hilda to lead the initiative, I suggested that we needed a small group of seven or eight Ipswich seniors who were basically keyboard literate. I vividly recall our next discussion when she rang (within the space of a week) and reported that she had identified seven seniors plus one who was only in his fifties but had a long white beard. My reaction was to declare him an honorary senior immediately. With the team of enthusiasts on board, all we needed to do was to secure the computing and communications equipment for their residences and get them online.

The SeniorNet project actually evolved as a joint venture between the Ipswich City Council and the Commonwealth Government's Department of Social Security. The Department of Social Security officially *loaned* the Ipswich City Council twelve very old very slow 386 machines which were about to be retired off. The Ipswich City Council was committed to providing all peripheral hardware and all continuing financial, technical, and administrative support. (This arrangement sounds like a typical agreement for local or state governments with the Federal government!) When the machines arrived, ten actually worked, and the other two were cannibalized for parts.[26] Two of the systems were installed in local regional retirement villages, and the remaining eight were installed in the private residences of the foundation group for SeniorNet.

For the people involved in the first few years of SeniorNet the impact was quite special. We did not just dump them in the middle of the great Pacific Ocean of information and wait to see if they could swim. We met with them as a group to identify their special interests, which ranged from palliative care, latchkey kids, and comparative religious

---

[25] Article by Peter Young of the *Sunday Mail,* February 1995.

[26] Interview with Darryl Cross, 10 September 2008, former GIL Development Manager.

studies to home brewed beer, great military battles, and classical music. We then introduced them to groups and web sites in other parts of the world where people shared the same interests. The reaction was galvanising. I have vivid recollection of the home brewing expert scarcely able to contain his excitement after discovering from someone in the UK about how he could double his output with each brew. There was another memorable experience involving a resident of a nursing home.[27]

> '. . . I can remember when we did the SeniorNet training going out to Colthorp Home on one occasion and receiving a big hug from a 102-year-old resident who said, "Thank you, Lindy, you have given me back the world" . . . this chap who had been locked in a dementia ward had during his life translated the Bible for the Baptist Church into multiple languages . . . he finished up on several Bulletin Boards arguing theology with the Hezbollah . . .'

After establishing connectivity with the Global Info-Links hub most of the necessary training was provided by Lindy McKeown and her colleagues from the education module. Marketing efforts were supported by Peter Gillard. Over the years numerous different state government agencies and local computer supply companies have provided further very tangible support.

In a formal sense back in 1996 Hilda des Arts and her colleagues defined the objectives of SeniorNet in the following manner:

- to promote companionship and social interaction among seniors aged fifty-five years and over, who share interests in learning computer literacy and communication using computers and the Internet
- to establish SeniorNet Training Centres to provide training courses in computer operating skills, including using the resources of the Internet
- to use computers as tools to integrate the generations by encouraging younger people, including members of high school student bodies, to become volunteer helpers and instructors for SeniorNet members on computer training courses
- to promote the SeniorNet organisation, so that it may spread across the nation, helping seniors keep pace with technology, thereby maintaining an effective lifestyle

Training and skills development has therefore been the serious focus of SeniorNet since its inception.

A snapshot of the training opportunities available currently includes the following:

---

[27]   Interview with Lindy McKeown, 12 September 2008.

Learning to Type
PowerPoint Q&A
Jazzy emails
Australian Genealogy
Creating Booklets in Word
My Pictures for Beginners
Blogging in Edgex
Printmaster e-Security
Photoshop Q&A
The Drawing Toolbar.

As an organisation Ipswich SeniorNet promotes links to Lets Talk Net, Silver Surfers, Silver Peers, ABC's of Computing, Computer Help for People Over Fifty, Internet Basics for Seniors, Grey Path, Seniors and the Internet, Seniors Enquiry Line, About Seniors, Council on the Aging, National Seniors Australia, Birds Down Under, and Recreation and Entertainment for Computer-using Seniors. All these online links have been developed subsequent to the work of the numerous volunteers who have made Ipswich SeniorNet a successful trail blazing organisation.

During the fifteen years since its establishment, Ipswich SeniorNet has provided skills development opportunities for several thousand people whose lives have been enriched as a result. When Hilda Des Arts died in 2002, she had achieved heroine status throughout Australia amongst the nation's senior citizens. Today the group in Ipswich proudly claims a membership of 350 people.

Businesses Online (eCommerce and the Business Module)

'. . . The secure payments system was at the very centre of the take off of eCommerce. Until there was a very secure system, eCommerce could never spread . . . it took years for people's fears to be allayed about actually paying online . . .'

Richard Naylor: Internet pioneer at the Wellington City Council New Zealand.
3 October 2008

Our preoccupation in 1994/5 with developing a new basis for the Ipswich economy meant that it was inevitable that a business module of Global Info-Links would constitute an important priority. Our quite extraordinary ambition to create the electronic marketplace was only about fifteen years before its time, and comprehensively beyond the capacity of one regional city. As a measure of our blind faith in the future it is worth remembering that in 1994 no business in Australia had a URL or presence on the World Wide Web. Precious few, if any, businesses had an Internet-based email address, and the first SMS text message was years away from being transmitted. In that somewhat pre-historic atmosphere, we were determined to lay some of the foundations for eCommerce.

In early 1995, we described the electronic market place as:[28]

- a new environment in which transactions occur and products and services are purchased (in some instances delivered) electronically
- a place for consumers to browse, locate, evaluate, and purchase goods and services
- an electronic gallery for business to promote their products and services to a global market of potential customers
- a platform for business development and innovation

---

[28]   'Ipswich 2010: Economic Development, Building on our Strengths', published by Ipswich City Council, 1995.

- a valuable information resource assembled from the thousands of World Wide Web pages that appear on the Internet

With the benefit of hindsight no single program by any agency of government was going to create the operational environment for eCommerce. It had to emerge globally almost like osmosis with all the highs and lows that one might expect of a major transformation in commercial behaviour. Even after the arrival of Amazon.com, eBay, and Google, eCommerce has yet to fully flower anywhere in the world. In the mid-1990s, we not only lacked the technology, we also lacked the critical mass of key people to drive eCommerce. All the business and organisational directories in the world were of limited relevance until literally millions of businesses and hundreds of millions of consumers were physically networked and could see the tangible benefits of operating in the new *marketspace.*

The transition from *marketplace* to *marketspace* was a major cultural challenge, the extent of which is only now properly understood in the ICT industry. It takes a few weeks or months to install new computing and telecommunications equipment in any organisation. However, it takes many years to achieve the cultural change that enables the same organisations to harness the full potential of the new technology.

One of the oldest and most practical definitions of eCommerce which we used in the early 1990s was[29]

> *. . . the application of the latest forms of communications and computing technologies to the five basic stages of the commercial process . . . namely*
>
> - *choosing goods and services,*
> - *ordering goods and services,*
> - *delivery of goods and services,*
> - *after-sales service, and*
> - *a payment system . . .*

In our very earliest pitches to business groups and associations, we emphasised the great benefits of doing business online as benefits for sales, purchasing, and the management of the business. In respect of sales we argued it was for wider markets, making it easier for customers to order, experiencing easier and more effective communications with customers, improved customer service, finding and contacting new customers, and finding out about the competition. In terms of purchasing, it was about getting better stuff, cheaper and faster, by finding new suppliers, products, and services, getting latest pricing and specification data, and placing and chasing orders. In terms of managing

---

[29]   Defined by the Global Info-Links team, 1995.

the business better it was about working smarter not harder with online access for payroll and taxation, real-time tracking of orders and shipments, and superior contact with customers.

eCommerce actually had its origins in the 1980s with a phenomenon known as EDI (Electronic Data Interchange), involving computer to computer exchange of electronic documents for contracts, forms, purchase orders, and invoicing. EDI was early technology; it involved vendor lock-in and proved to be expensive, not particularly user-friendly and clumsy. As a result, eCommerce stalled in the mid to late 1980s.

The period 1991-4 proved to be a major watershed for eCommerce with the development and release of the World Wide Web and the Mosaic and Netscape web browsers. Suddenly, there was an attractive, user-friendly interface for the Internet. The interest of the public was suddenly stimulated. Contrary to the hopes of the Internet purists, the first Internet business transactions occurred in 1994/5.

At a typical 'Doing Business on the Internet' workshop for local businesses in Ipswich in early 1996, we extolled the virtues of being online by reciting what we then believed were the top ten reasons to connect:

1. Communicate more effectively using interactive graphic formats.
2. Improve the speed and accuracy of communications using internal and global email.
3. Reduce the total cost of communications.
4. Reduce the cost of customer support and relationship management.
5. Increase the reach of communications channels.
6. Increase the utilisation of organisational content.
7. Conduct formal and informal market research.
8. Broaden the media reach of the organisation.
9. Learn from the new media.
10. Improve options available to the organisation.

Awareness seminars designed to demystify the Internet, and identify new opportunities continued for some years. Case studies of early success stories were highly popular. Within three years of opening, Global Info-Links had 4,000 business accounts and was hosting more than three hundred and fifty business web sites. In fulfilling part of its new brief the Ipswich Global Information Centre developed a special online business research service for local businesses. This was clearly a world-class innovation to have a city library (in 1995) actively supporting, if not leading, the introduction of eCommerce by:

- undertaking online research and document delivery to local businesses
- developing a directory of Ipswich businesses on the web

- creating a 'business collection' of business/management books, videos, and online links for local businesses
- selecting and providing access to business-related databases and news wires

An informal survey of new employment opportunities conducted by the Global Info-Links management team in early 1996 revealed that new occupations in web building, web maintenance, system installation support and backup services, electronic publishing, multimedia, training specialists and providers, and information research and analysis were appearing. Whilst there was no radical transformation of business practice overnight in 1995/6, local business was well positioned when eCommerce took off in the years that followed.

In the decade after the mid-1990s four major categories of eCommerce evolved: business to consumer eCommerce, (B2C), business to business eCommerce (B2B), consumer to consumer eCommerce (C2C), and consumer to business eCommerce (C2B).

Despite the initial significance of business to consumer eCommerce, by far the most significant form of eCommerce today is business to business activity. This is also the field which is expected to experience the most explosive growth in the future with the roll-out of high-capacity broadband infrastructure.

Local, State, and Federal Government Services Online

'... Global Info-Links was a tremendous boost to the community and took away the whole notion of a strictly blue-collar community. I think it ultimately got us the University of Queensland campus here in Ipswich ...'

Cathy Watson, Ipswich City Council Library Operations Manager,
a senior librarian at Ipswich since 1994.
15 September 2008

In 1994, very few state and Federal government agencies in Australia had a web site. When the Global Info-Links web committee started work on the web site for Ipswich city and GIL (September to November 1994), we could find no other community web sites in Australia. Given the limitations on our search tools at the time, we were unable to find a community web site in North America or Europe. We were aware of endeavours to hard-wire Blacksburg, Virginia, but we were unable to discover a web site as such. As a consequence, we had to design the first template for such a site. As rudimentary as it now appears, the site map which was approved by the GIL Web Committee on 8 November 1994 incorporated the following features:[30]

The Ipswich Web
- The beginner's guide to exploring this web site, using
  - Mosaic
  - Lynx

- Web Index
- What's new on the Web
- Disclaimer

---

[30] Minutes of the Global Info-Links Web Committee, 1994.

Global Info-Links

- The Global Info-Links Project
- Global Info-Links Services
- Frequently asked questions about Global Info-Links

Global Info-Links Special Electronic Services

Initially a short, one page document, but after March 1995 a multi part document as follows:

- GIL Special Electronic Services
- Subscribing to GIL's special electronic Services
- Launch of the GIL special electronic services on the Internet
- The pro active role of the software developer
- Benefits of establishing a software office in Ipswich
- Information delivered free to your screen
- Online services to support a range of business and community groups
- Runtime programs delivered through FTP to your screen
- The support role of the Ipswich Librarians
- Other services

Ipswich City Information

- A message from the Mayor
- Meet the City councillors
- A message from the CEO of the Ipswich City Council
- Ipswich City
  - o Ipswich past and present
  - o The City's vision for the future
  - o Where in the world is Ipswich
  - o Professorile Australia and Queensland
  - o Ipswich Heritage City

- Ipswich City Council Documents:
  - o Ipswich City Corporate Plan
  - o Ipswich City and region Cultural Development Policy
  - o Minutes of last Council meeting (fortnightly; keep 2 most recent)
  - o Ipswich City Council Quality Manual
  - o The Ipswich City Council 1994/95 Financial Budget

- Ipswich Events Calendar

- Ipswich City and Region Community Guide
- Directory of services for seniors in Ipswich
- Ipswich Global Information Centre

Tourism, Recreation, and Leisure
- Ipswich Events Calendar

Education Employment and Training
- Directory of educational institutions in Ipswich Region
- External link to the Australian Bureau of Statistics
- External Link to the Department of Social Security
- External link to the Queensland Department of Primary Industry
- Educational Resources on the Internet

Business and Economic Development
- Link to Ipswich City page (why business should invest in this region)
- Key Economic Organisations
- Australian Bureau of Statistics (external link)
- Department of social Security (external link)
- Department of Primary Industry (external link)

Rural Information
- Department of Primary Industry (external link)

Exploring the Internet
- What is the Internet
- How to use the Internet
  - Basic instructions on how to use the Internet including Mosaic, Lynx, email, newsreaders, telnet, gopher, and ftp
  - Links to information about using other sites; including Scout Report, InterNic InfoGuide, and electronic frontier foundation.

- How to find other material on the Internet, bookshops, university libraries and the Global Information Centre.
- Links to Internet searching tools such as Web crawler and World Wide Web Worm.
- Links to some interesting World Wide Webs.

Our efforts to secure a screen grab of the very first (1994 version) of the Ipswich/Global Info-Links home page have been unsuccessful. To the best of our knowledge global archives that have records of the very earliest websites only go back to 1996. Sadly, at the time we were not sufficiently focussed on the significance of what we were doing.

In the decade that followed the mid-1990s there was a veritable explosion in the demand for websites for government agencies, commercial organisations, educational institutions, and a wide range of community groups. In the early years, government agencies competed to outdo each other and included bells and whistles that rendered many websites quite useless. Government agencies, where budgets for website work became increasingly generous, appeared oblivious to the fact that many parts of the community lacked both the technology and skills base to effectively use their masterpieces. This seemed to be a learning curve we just had to experience. Led by the government of Victoria, most Australian governments eventually set deadlines after which many categories of essential government information could only be accessed on the Web. Cost shifting associated with transactions and printing documents became increasingly attractive. At the end of the first decade of the twenty-first century, agencies and departments of government in Australia have millions of pages of content on the Web. An entire new industry was spawned to feed what virtually became an insatiable demand for the Web presence.

A University Campus for Ipswich:
The Twin Project

'. . . Make no mistake, without Global Info-Links we would not have a university in this city . . .'

Dave Underwood, former MLA for Ipswich West (1977-89) and
former Mayor of Ipswich (1991-5).
2 November 2008

The design and development of Global Info-Links and the establishment of a university campus in Ipswich were implemented from the very beginning of the economic turnaround strategy for Ipswich in 1992 as twin projects.[31] Global Info-Links which was implemented by the Ipswich City Council in its own right took two years to design and construct. The university project which depended heavily on the cooperation of Federal and state governments and the University of Queensland took seven years to implement. In the operational sense within the Ipswich City Council both projects were managed by the Development Investment Group and generously supported by the Planning Group and R & D Group of the Council. Both projects were designed to provide foundations for a local economy connected to the Global Knowledge Economy of the twenty-first century. Both were seen as important components of the economy needed to minimise Ipswich's dependence on the old industrial world.

Reviewing the first five years of the life of UQ, Ipswich campus, in 2004, the vice-chancellor, Professor John Hay, was quoted inter alia as saying,[32]

> *'. . . We are steadily building a global reputation for our innovative courses, ultra modern teaching, and gracefully restored heritage-listed buildings . . .*

---

[31]   Ipswich City Council minutes. Memos from the IDIM which marked the beginning of both projects were written on, 10 December 1992.

[32]   *The Road to UQ Ipswich,* The University of Queensland, 2004.

*located in one of the most e conscious cities in Queensland. UQ Ipswich has
one of the best student to computer ratios in the country . . . the University of
Queensland was one of the first universities in Australia to build a completely
Web-enabled campus from scratch . . .'*

For those of us involved in developing the twin projects, the vice-chancellor's comments
came as no surprise.

It is a matter of record that the idea of establishing a university in Ipswich had been
mooted on a number of occasions during the one hundred and thirty-six years that
followed the launch of the Ipswich Grammar School in 1863. Until 1992 there was no
concerted action group or plan to achieve this important goal for the city. When the
commitment was made by the Ipswich City Council in 1992/3 the concept for the first
time had the staffing and funding support to become a serious initiative rather than a
dream about which people opined from time to time.

For the express purpose of establishing a university in Ipswich the Ipswich City Council
formed a taskforce of prominent local citizens backed up by the IDI Group.

The university taskforce was formally established, and its first meeting held at the
Ipswich City Council on 5 February 1993. The membership of the original taskforce
comprised Ald Dave Underwood (Chairman), Mr Mal Bryce, IDIM (Convener and
Project Manager), Mr Neville Bonner (Former Senator for Queensland), Mr Tom
Edwards (Ipswich Businessman), Mr David Hamill, MLA (state MP for Ipswich), Mrs
Sarah Israel (Business Development Manager for the Ipswich Regional Development
Corporation), Mr Les Scott, MHR (Federal Member for Oxley), Ald. Paul Tully (Ipswich
City Council), and Dr David Warner (Director of the Ipswich TAFE College). It was
of immense importance to the work of the taskforce that David Hamill as the local
member for Ipswich became a senior minister in the Queensland State Government in
the years that followed. David played a direct role in convincing the federal government
to provide the capital dollars for a new campus in Queensland, and he would probably
describe as a modest role his efforts to convince the Queensland State Government to
locate that new campus in Ipswich.

Messrs Leon Rose, Paul Moody, John Brannock, Graham Isbell, and Ian McGregor
were added to the taskforce during 1993. In the long haul to 1996, the membership of
the taskforce was further expanded.

Marie Kavanagh and Bruce Prideaux, both of whom lived in Ipswich and worked as lecturers
at the UQ Gatton Campus, agreed to act as consultants/advisors to the taskforce. The Ipswich
City Council Taskforce support group included the IDIM, the Strategic Planner (John
Adams), and Garth Moore, Linwood Rae, Paula Watkins, and Matthew McKerrow.

The first business of the taskforce was to 'develop the case' for establishing a university in Ipswich after which a campaign would be undertaken to identify a Queensland university interested in coming to Ipswich and then the source of funding for the project.

Early in the deliberations of the taskforce it became clear that there were a number of options to be considered in defining the scope and nature of a new campus that would open its doors in the late 1990s, i.e. would it be a fully integrated campus independent of other universities (e.g. a University of Ipswich), a specialised campus of an existing university, a feeder campus, a Community College, or even the hub of a new Open University. Commonwealth government funding policy at the time clearly favoured the development of regional campuses of existing universities which made use of existing expertise and infrastructure. This reality virtually determined that any university (other than a private university) to be established in Ipswich in the 1990s would be a regional campus of an existing university. There were four universities in South East Queensland with a potential interest in establishing a campus in Ipswich namely, The University of Queensland, The Queensland University of Technology, Griffith University, and The University of Southern Queensland based in Toowoomba.

Our first choice institution was the University of Queensland because it had long-standing links with the Ipswich TAFE College and had clear interests (including the Gatton College) in the Western Corridor. The Queensland University of Technology when approached showed no interest in Ipswich and preferred to concentrate on its commitments to the north of Brisbane. The leadership team from Griffith University expressed a positive interest and visited Ipswich. Eventually, they decided to concentrate their resources on a new campus they were developing at Logan city. The University of Southern Queensland expressed a positive response but lacked the resources to tackle the challenge.

By the end of 1993 it was clear that the University of Queensland was interested and prepared to establish a new campus essentially funded by the Commonwealth government in the Western Corridor in the vicinity of Ipswich. The question that then consumed three years in the answering was 'Precisely, which site should be chosen for the campus?'

In the first instance there was a choice to be made between Springfield and Ipswich city. Springfield was a greenfield site within the Moreton Shire Council boundaries[33] about to be developed by the MUR Property Group involving 14,000 lots and a potential population of approximately 40-50,000 people. In October 1991, the University of Queensland was offered an option on a site of eighty hectares to develop a campus in Springfield. Eventually, the lack of services and associated infrastructure such as

---

[33]   In May 1995, Moreton Shire Council and Ipswich City Council were merged into the one local governing authority.

transport, roads, water, sewerage, and telecommunications made the Springfield option less attractive to the university and the state government.

Within Ipswich city, four sites were originally identified as possibilities for a future university campus. The first was the Ipswich TAFE College in Bundamba which would have involved an interesting co-location concept. The second, Redbank Rifle Range was effectively another greenfield site which was also discounted early in the piece because of infrastructure issues. The third site was the Challinor Centre in central Ipswich, which had been built in 1887 as a hospital for patients with mental illness. In 1968, it was renamed Challinor and for the next thirty years provided residential care for people with intellectual disabilities and psychiatric illnesses. Despite the remarkably attractive real estate setting, the university taskforce did not believe any university would be interested in taking over and redeveloping a site that had been a place of such tragedy and sadness for more than a hundred years.

The fourth site was the North Ipswich Railway Workshops which after very lengthy consideration became the site preferred by the Ipswich University taskforce, the Ipswich City Council, and the government of Queensland. In its formal presentation to the University of Queensland, in November 1993, the Ipswich University taskforce outlined its logic as mentioned below:

- it involved fifty-seven hectares with two kilometres of river frontage
- Q Rail was preparing to leave the site and consolidate its facilities in Redbank
- to the north and east of the site there were areas of low-density and low-cost housing
- the city of Ipswich agreed to add a further adjoining ten hectares of recreational land at Woodend
- all existing buildings were above the one-in-hundred-year flood level
- the site was serviced by a water supply and sewerage system which had recently been upgraded
- there was easy access to major and arterial roads
- the site had rail line access and was serviced by an excellent bus service
- it was located within easy walking and cycling distance of the town centre

All sites were owned by the Queensland government and potentially available for redevelopment as a university.

During 1994 and 1995 a number of important developments occurred at a grinding pace. The Federal government confirmed the availability of funding for capital works and student places for a campus in the Western Corridor. The state government confirmed its preference for Ipswich as the location of the university campus. The state government formally offered the University of Queensland the North Ipswich Railway Workshops as a site. The Office of Property and Facilities and the Office of Buildings and Grounds at the University of Queensland mounted a rearguard action of opposition to the North Ipswich site.[34] In June 1995, the University of Queensland announced its preference for the Challinor Centre as the site for a campus and formally rejected the offer of North Ipswich. A serious tug of war between the University of Queensland and the state Government over the most appropriate site for the campus then ensued for eighteen months. Finally, the university won the tug of war and announced on the 10 December 1996 that it would proceed to establish a university campus in Ipswich at the Challinor Centre. The following day the Queensland Times in Ipswich ran a front page headline that read:

'GIL NETS UNIVERSITY FOR IPSWICH'

In that front page story the vice-chancellor of the University of Queensland Professor John Hay was quoted as saying,

> '. . . That Global Info-Links was a major factor in the decision to come to Ipswich and in the design of courses to be offered at the new campus . . .'

Supporting the same interesting observation, the UQ Registrar, Douglas Porter, was quoted as saying,

> '. . . an Ipswich campus made all sorts of sense especially in the light of the Smart City planning and the city's transformation from an industrial community . . .'

University of Queensland historian, Judith Nissan, went so far as to suggest,

> '. . . Global Info-Links played a key part in the city's technology-led recovery. GIL was launched when few Australians were aware of the Internet or its likely impact. This example of applied information technology in action was a draw card for the University of Queensland . . .'[35]

In February 1997, the taskforce was wound up and a new group 'The UQ Ipswich City Support Group' was established. This group was subsequently reconstituted as the 'Friends of UQ Ipswich' in June 1998.

---

[34]   Judith Nissen: *The Road to UQ Ipswich,* The University of Queensland, Page 15.
[35]   IBID

The official opening of UQ Ipswich occurred on 22 June 1999. The inaugural student intake occurred in February 2000.

A decade later, the University of Queensland, Ipswich Campus, has approximately eighteen hundred students and three hundred and ten staff, two hundred and twenty of whom are full time. From 2001-9 a total of 2,438 students were graduated, and capital dollars invested in developing the campus exceeded $57 million. The key theme of academic courses run and/or research conducted at the campus now focuses on health sciences, including nursing, medicine, health administration, and dietetics. In respect of the future development of the city, the university campus has clearly had a catalytic effect. Works commenced in early 2010 to co-locate Bremer State High School to a site immediately adjoining the Ipswich University of Queensland campus. Involving year's eleven to twelve students, this will mean a significant change to the nature of the campus and the precinct with important implications for transport and traffic. In 2009, the federal government announced approval for a GP Super Clinic which will bring large numbers of people to the UQ Ipswich Campus for treatment. It will also add impetus to the argument of the University for the relocation of the Ipswich Hospital to the campus. Probably the most ambitious and innovative of new developments for the campus involves plans for a University College, which will deliver a range of programs across a variety of subject areas leading to the award of an Associate Degree. The college will incorporate tertiary preparation and bridging programs and the provision of alternative education pathways for students who initially fail to meet the standards for direct entry to UQ.

With predictions that the population of the city of Ipswich could reach 450,000 within twenty years, the university campus may well prove to be in the right place at the right time.

Lindy McKeown (left) and
Poppy Masselos (right).

Two highly talented professionals who were amongst the first teachers in the world to introduce the Internet to the classroom.

The brave new world 1994. The enthusiasm for the Internet was infectious.

Photo: Courtesy of Lyle Radford

Dr Hilda Des Arts, inaugural Chair of Ipswich SeniorNet who led Ipswich senior citizens into cyber space in 1994; before the world knew that cyber space existed.

Photo: Courtesy of Lyle Radford

Stage One for the Ipswich Campus of the University of Queensland 1998.

Photo: Courtesy of the University of Queensland.

Citizens of Ipswich being introduced to the Internet at the Ipswich Global Information Centre, November 1994.

Photo: Courtesy of Lyle Radford

First Orientation Day for UQ Ipswich. February 1999. The beginnings of a new campus community in Ipswich.

Photo: Courtesy of the University of Queensland.

Former Ipswich CEO Jamie Quinn, (right) and Mayor of Ipswich Paul Pisasale, (left) proudly holding the 2007 LivCom Award; awarded to Ipswich as the "World's Most Liveable City with a population between 75,000 and 200,000".

PART 4

THE FUTURE

- The Ipswich InfoCity Plan and the Broadband Economy

The Ipswich InfoCity Plan and the Broadband Economy

'. . . The demise of DISTANCE as the key to the cost of communications may well prove to be the most significant economic force shaping the next half century . . .'

'The Revolution Begins at Last', The Economist, 30 September 1995

When the article referred to above was drawn to our attention at the end of 1995 very few people appreciated how prophetic it would turn out to be. The entire online revolution which has so fundamentally changed the economy of the world in the last fifteen years depended upon our ability to defeat distance as the key determinant of the cost of telecommunications services. By the end of the 1990s the cost of delivering sophisticated online services was virtually independent of geography. Perhaps more than any other economic force, dramatic reductions in the cost of telecommunications services was the true enabler of globalisation. With the benefits of hindsight there are no doubt keen observers who would suggest that the savagely debilitating global financial crisis from which the world is still struggling to recover, may never have occurred without super fast, super cheap, and super reliable telecommunication services.

The Ipswich InfoCity Plan

In 2008 the Ipswich City Council launched an exciting and comprehensive economic development plan (2009-31) for the city. The core of the strategy involves four pillars: city leadership, regional leadership, city growth, and city competitiveness. The specific areas in which the city intends to establish its leadership role include ICT leadership, the development of the city CBD, and sustainable development. In this latest Economic Development Plan[36] it is clearly articulated that the city intends to reclaim its leadership role in ICT for the purpose of further developing the digital innovation community. The document spells out the vision of the InfoCity Plan:

---

[36]   Economic Development Plan for Ipswich City, 2009-31, page 13, published by the Ipswich City Council

'... *Ipswich City will be a leading digital community in Australia. The InfoCity Plan will create a digital innovation community that involves and benefits the wider community and provides the base for innovation and industry leadership in digital technology ...*'

The specific goals of the plan are to:

- establish next generation broadband infrastructure throughout the city
- create communities that use this infrastructure to its best advantage
- encourage through examples and case studies increased participation in digital solutions in education, business, and the community at large

The dream of hard-wiring the city of Ipswich for super-fast broadband capability was a dream we had in 1995 and 1996 for Stage 3 of Global Info-Links. The dream ended fairly abruptly in 1995 when the Federal government of the day failed to share the dream and declined our application for the funding[37] to hard-wire between 500 and 1,000 points in the Ipswich CBD. Fifteen years later leaders of commercial and government organisations worldwide are aware that serious benefits can and will be derived from rolling out high-capacity broadband telecommunications infrastructure, i.e. FTTP.

This reality has not been lost on the Ipswich City Council.

The Broadband Economy

For more than a hundred years after the world's first telephone call in 1876, bandwidth for residential connections was not an issue of any significance because traditional telecommunications infrastructure was designed and built to handle voice traffic. With the switch from the use of analogue to digital technologies in the 1980s the flow of data traffic increased dramatically.

The word broadband only entered common usage at the end of the 1990s when the demand for online delivery of video and graphic-intensive images became substantial. What had been developed for a telephone service was by then expected to carry data, voice, and video traffic.

The demand for high-definition, interactive video for business, professional, and recreational purposes has clearly emerged as the key application which now drives the demand for high-capacity broadband infrastructure.

---

[37] The Ipswich City Council had applied for $100,000 to undertake a detailed feasibility study.

Definitions of broadband are many and varied. Some experts define broadband by speed and others by functionality. Conventional definitions of broadband tend to focus on what it is not, rather than what it is.[38] There is general agreement that today's distinction between narrowband and broadband is the transmission capacity equal to or above 256 Kbps. There is, however, no upper limit placed on what broadband can become, and there is widespread evidence to suggest that broadband speeds and its performance to price ratio are doubling every fifteen to eighteen months. Broadband is also defined as a service that is always on, where price is distance independent and which is basically available without limitations on the use of capacity. A third important aspect of broadband is that it is both fixed and mobile. In a high-capacity broadband network, the term broadband will refer to the quality of the access environment and the possibilities this allows rather than whether a user is connected to a fixed line or wireless environment at any particular time. A sobering reality about future demand for bandwidth is that the main users of broadband will not necessarily be humans but increasingly machines and objects that are interconnected and controlled in a ubiquitous network.

In Australia, the original official definition developed by the ACCC in 2002 was

> '. . . *Any high-speed connection to the Internet greater than 200 Kbps in the last mile over a mix of media . . .*'

At the end of the December Quarter, 2007, the Australian Bureau of Statistics reported that there were in Australia:

- 7.1 million connections to the Internet
- 2 million still using dial-up access
- 1.6 million who had speeds up to 0.5 Mbps
- 1.2 million who had speeds between 0.5 and 1.5 Mbps
- 1 million who had speeds between 1.5 and 8 Mbps
- only 1.3 million who enjoyed speeds > 8 Mbps

The Internet has become an indispensable communications tool and information resource for businesses, governments, community organisations, individuals, and families. During this first decade of the twenty-first century, the proliferation of broadband access to the Internet has changed business practices, consumer behaviour, the nature of entertainment, types of employment, and the basics of education and research, and health service delivery.

---

[38] D'Costa and Kelly: 'Broadband as a platform for Economic Development', OECD Conference on Innovation and Sustainable Growth in a Globalized World, Paris, November 2008.

By 2008, more than 180 economies worldwide had launched broadband services. Globally the number of subscribers had surpassed 500 million (including fixed and mobile broadband subscribers).[39]

The incremental benefits of high-capacity broadband over the current generation of broadband flow directly from the enhanced user experience and services it can support. These in turn are heavily influenced by the key attributes of high-capacity networks such as:

- higher download and particularly higher upload speeds and lower unit costs
- reduced waiting time for information
- a significant reduction in faults
- greater consistency of bandwidth across users
- the ability to cannibalise the traditional businesses of other service providers, for example, live TV and traditional telephone services
- lower latency, lower error rate, and freedom from radiofrequency interference[40]

On a global scale, sophisticated nations, regions, and communities are actively involved in pursuit of the very real economic, environmental, and social benefits associated with the broadband economy.

Economic Benefits of High-capacity Broadband

High-capacity broadband is the infrastructure on which twenty-first century business will be built. Ipswich with its track record and experience can be a part of this phenomenon.

Top quality telecommunications services are important to businesses of all sizes, from large manufacturers managing their global supply chain, to mid-sized retail and service-based businesses connecting to customers, the home-based consultant, or eBay business.

High-capacity broadband infrastructure is now the driver of great significance that will power a sustained upturn and the next long-term wave of development in the global economy. This phase of the ICT (information and communication technology) revolution is comparable to the impact of steam and rail technology (1820s), steel and electricity (1870s), and automobiles, oil, and mass production after 1908.

---

[39]   ITU World Telecommunications Indicators Database, 2008.

[40]   Report for the Broadband Stakeholder Group: A Framework for evaluating the value of next-generation broadband, June 2008.

In the past, technological breakthroughs of such significance have been described as General Purpose Technology (GPT) enablers, responsible for long waves of innovation and economic growth frequently lasting for fifty to sixty years.[41]

As the technology continues to evolve and bandwidth increases, the scope for broadband to act as an enabler of structural change in the economy expands.

Broadband does not act on the economy in isolation, but as a complement to other information technologies. It has become the critical enabler for the use of computer-based applications that need to communicate. Many of these applications change the behaviour and productivity of both firms and individuals.

Telecommunications infrastructure has become an integral part of almost every aspect of the knowledge economy.[42] Public infrastructure increasingly depends on broadband communications networks for significant functions including traffic light control, control of sewerage systems, air traffic control as well as maritime and rail transport and logistics management systems. Many aspects of business are already taking place over broadband networks, such as supply chain management, fleet management, e-procurement, e-invoicing, online recruitment, customer service, call centres, online payment systems, eCommerce, co-ordination of fragmented production processes, and the connection of teleworkers to their employers. Consumers have also made great use of broadband networks for eCommerce, online payment systems, online reservations, online auctions, and online entertainment services.

The links between the existence of high-capacity broadband and the performance of the local, regional, and national economy are well documented. The essential links include opportunities for innovation, increased productivity growth, the special impact of eCommerce, the impact on telework programs and tele-presence facilities and the positive benefits for SMEs.

The Federal government through the Department of Broadband, Communications, and the Digital Economy is currently undertaking consultations on the future of the digital economy,[43] indicating their recognition of its importance across the Australian economy.

---

[41] Carlota Perez: *Technological Revolutions and Financial Capital*, Edward Elgar, UK, 2005.

[42] OECD Ministerial Background Report: For a ministerial meeting on the future of the Internet economy, Seoul Korea, June 2008.

[43] http://www.dbcde.gov.au/communications_for_business/industry_development/digital_economy

Opportunities for Innovation in Ipswich

Worldwide, broadband infrastructure has had a major beneficial impact on innovation. As a regional city with a well-earned reputation for innovation, Ipswich could expect to enjoy a competitive edge if the roll-out and exploitation of high-capacity broadband is carefully planned.

Broadband in association with other key ICTs has made it easier to uncover and develop good ideas and easier to create new products and services.

The most direct way in which ICTs boost innovation is by giving researchers more powerful tools for doing research. Broadband is the infrastructure that adds value to the tool box and facilitates the vital forms of interaction in effective innovation.

Virtual product development at geographically dispersed locations now allows researchers to model the operational properties of a product without having to build expensive prototypes. Whereas once R & D was virtually the sole preserve of large corporations, computers and the Internet have made it practical for SMEs to participate and compete.

The ICT tool box has made it possible for users and customers to become involved in development, design, and product innovation. Broadband has become the world's knowledge conduit, making it possible for innovators to learn faster than ever before what other innovators are doing and what level of opportunity the market offers.

Global knowledge management has become a reality rather than a theoretical possibility as a result of broadband infrastructure and a whole new generation of knowledge management tools and technologies that enable collaboration.

Broadband has made it practical and more cost-effective to run a network of geographically dispersed facilities to enforce standards of operation, branding, and all other aspects of successful marketing. It also enables concurrent R & D on multiple projects in different locations.

Broadband has made it possible for companies of all sizes to efficiently access talented people which are a vital key to successful innovation.

In his recently published book on broadband economies, Robert Bell very vividly states, . . . '*Broadband has become to innovation what fertilizer is to farming: a heady booster of performance . . .*'[44]

---

[44] Robert Bell, 'Broadband Economies. Creating the Community of the 21st Century', Intelligent Community Forum, NY.

Ipswich As a Place Where Productivity Is High

Productivity growth, which is the increase in the amount of output produced by workers per given unit of effort, is generally regarded as the most important measure and determinant of economic performance. Any community founded on high-capacity broadband is a community where productivity could be expected to be of the highest order.

There is now a strong consensus amongst economists that the ICT revolution incorporating broadband infrastructure was and continues to be responsible for the lion's share of the post-1995 rebound in productivity growth amongst developed economies. The implications of this view are significant given that the roll-out of high-capacity broadband infrastructure is still in its infancy. The switch to broadband services has produced massive cost savings at the level of the firm. At the same time the new networks have beneficial impacts on process efficiency, work organisation, procurement costs, product quality, and customer service.

The primary contribution of ICTs (incorporating broadband) in boosting productivity within the firm is by employees being more productive and thereby enabling the same number of employees to produce more products and provide more services. Sophisticated telecommunications networks together with other information technologies boost productivity by:

- enabling employees to do more things at the same time
- assisting employees to focus more exclusively on valuable work and avoid less productive distractions
- allowing routine tasks to be automated and remotely managed, where appropriate
- enabling firms to restructure their supply chains
- facilitating more productive self service
- allowing bits to be substituted for atoms
- enabling the creation of markets and market signals where before there were none
- helping markets to be more efficient by expanding consumer information

ICTs not only enable the creation of larger markets, they allow companies to achieve greater economies of scale and exert greater competitive pressure on firms to boost performance. They also give managers better tools by which to make decisions. Shorter product cycles, rapidly changing economic environments, and a multitude of new competitors means that decision-makers must make decisions faster and with more accuracy than ever before.[45]

---

[45]   Atkinson and McKay: 'Digital Prosperity', IT and Innovation Foundation, March 2007.

As broadband spreads throughout the economy, transformations are taking place in the way business is done, work is organised, and resources are allocated. These effects are most noticeable in the service sector of the economy in areas such as financial services, business services, transportation, real estate, travel and tourism, retail, and communication services.

The Role of eCommerce in Ipswich

The City of Ipswich was one of the world's leading pioneers of eCommerce in the early 1990s. It seems appropriate that Ipswich now has the opportunity to enjoy the fruits of the next generation of eCommerce.

The most readily identified benefits or advantages of eCommerce which will be further enhanced by the development of high-capacity broadband are that companies:

- become more efficient and flexible in their internal operations
- are able to work more closely with their suppliers
- can be more responsive to the needs and expectations of their customers
- can select the best suppliers regardless of location
- can sell to an expanded global market
- can benefit from better management systems across different organisations

Modern telecommunication services and technology were therefore at the heart of eCommerce from its inception. eCommerce emerged and grew in quite a phenomenal way after 1994 on the basis of narrowband dial-up connections to the Internet.

A very rudimentary form of broadband appeared in 1998 with the release in North America of DSL (Digital Subscriber Line) technology and the rapid growth of eCommerce followed.

Whilst eCommerce still represents only a minor percentage of total commerce, effectively breaking the sound barrier with high-capacity broadband is expected to introduce the next dramatic chapter in the development of eCommerce.

Telework and Tele-Presence Facilities in Ipswich

By virtue of its geographical location Ipswich could emerge as a model for other Australian regional telework centres. Situated 45 kms from the Brisbane CBD, Ipswich would be ideally positioned to become the key Telework centre in South East Queensland.

116

The earliest telework initiatives associated with 'home-based work' date back to the 1960s and 1970s. Like many of the important outcomes of the ICT revolution telework had a long gestation period. Apart from pioneering efforts, serious telework programs did not get underway until the 1990s.[46] As with eCommerce, telework arrangements emerged in association with narrowband infrastructure in the first half of the 1990s and accelerated substantially with the arrival of early stage broadband in 1998.

Future implications for telework with the development of high-capacity broadband are expected to be of major significance.

There are different interpretations of the concept of telework. In this report telework is understood to mean work that relies on ICTs, especially telecommunications infrastructure to be carried out from remote locations. Worldwide it is generally accepted as a work arrangement in which employees regularly work at an alternate worksite such as the employees' homes, a telecommuting centre, or other alternate site.

Although a great deal of discussion had been had about the differences between telework, telecommuting, and flexiplace, for the purposes of this book these terms will be treated as synonyms.

Tele-presence facilities are contemporary videoconferencing systems and services that use virtual reality techniques to much more closely emulate real face-to-face interactions. The concept/product has been developed to provide high-definition video, spatial audio, and a physical setup designed to link two separated rooms to resemble a single conference room. The facilities commenced as single point-to-point operations but have developed into multipoint facilities. Worldwide they are a classic indicator of future business opportunities and changed business practices made possible by the availability of high-capacity broadband.

The amount of work carried out 'in the field', the types of contractual arrangements and the technology applied vary greatly from place to place and amongst sectors of the economy.

Broadband connections are greatly increasing flexibility and productivity of teleworking employees. Prime examples include situations where people make phone calls and check emails while travelling or while waiting. Companies are also starting to save costs on office space and office overheads as the design of office space changes to reflect the new more flexible working arrangements. Other tangible, widely recognised economic benefits of effective teleworking include the following:

---

[46]   Dr Wendell Joice: 'The Evolution of Telework in the Federal Government', US Office of General Services Administration, 2000.

- reduced costs associated with staff relocation and recruitment
- improved motivation of the workforce
- retention of key skilled employees
- multi-disciplinary teams can be assembled irrespective of geography
- greater organisational resilience in the face of external disruptions
- enhanced customer service, beyond normal working hours
- reduced costs associated with travel time
- reduced traffic congestion
- wider employment/work opportunities
- greater access to work for people with specific difficulties

In contemporary terms, the essential enabling technologies required by teleworkers include laptop computers, mobile phones, broadband Internet connection, and access to the company's network. There is increasing evidence to suggest that in the foreseeable future, the 'must have' technology (which highlights the importance of high-capacity broadband) for teleworkers will be the IP Virtual Private Network (VPN) which replicates the office environment at a remote location.

Small- and Medium-Sized Enterprises in Ipswich

Although Ipswich features a significant number of several large employment generators, the vast majority of all businesses to be established in and near Ipswich in the future will be small- and medium-sized Enterprises (SMEs). SMEs are in many respects the engine room of all economies. They represent a very high proportion of all businesses, provide employment opportunities for more than 65 percent of all employees, and are an invaluable training ground for business operators across numerous aspects of the economy. Many small- and medium-sized businesses were slow to adopt ICTs in the 1990s for a range of reasons. However, by the turn of the century a vast majority of Australian SMEs were online and were beginning to realise the benefits of the Internet economy, albeit by very ordinary speeds of connection.

Across a significant number of sectors of the economy, SMEs are deriving a range of very important benefits of broadband connectivity which are as follows:

- evolving supply chain management with partners who demand on-line integration
- introducing new collaborative working tools to enhance efficiency
- providing flexible working arrangements to retain key employees
- Improving customer relationship management to meet and exceed customer expectations for sales and support
- outsourcing activities to save costs
- aggregating content to achieve efficiency gains

- linking the mobile workforce with the company and its data resources

As with so many other parts of the economy, the introduction of high-capacity broadband will enable SMEs to save valuable additional time, do more of selected important things, and engage in a whole new range of new activities.

An Environmental Edge for Ipswich

In recent years major international studies have demonstrated the links between high-capacity broadband telecommunications networks and the ability to significantly reduce greenhouse gas emissions. It appears that the greatest potential for greenhouse reductions are to be found in eCommerce applications, telecommuting, teleconferencing, and paper reductions.[47]

If Ipswich is to be presented to the world as an environmentally friendly community, high-capacity broadband is essential.

Broadband infrastructure has emerged as a critical element of infrastructure as communities the world over strive for a 'low carbon' future. Links between serious bandwidth and changes to the way people and businesses live, shop, travel, work, and use products are an important part of the immediate future. The consumption of oil and other fossil fuels has created a serious air and water pollution challenge. At the same time the human population of the globe is increasing and the planet's biodiversity is dwindling. ICTs (especially broadband networks) are making a major contribution to our understanding of the natural environment and humanity's impact upon it.

As scientific effort becomes more sophisticated, the demand for bandwidth increases.

In a substantial number of fields, critical collaboration and remote management of data gathering (made possible by high-quality high-capacity broadband) is helping to mitigate today's pressing environmental issues.

The Concept of Decentralised Workplaces for Ipswich

Telecommuting and telework have been defined previously. The de-centralised workplace is a variation on teleworking and is the ability of people to work not at home but close to home at a telework centre.

Access to such a facility can significantly reduce commuting distances, travel time, and transport emissions. The concept of the de-centralised workplace may involve

---

[47]   Joseph P Fuhr: Broadband Services Report, American Consumer Institute, October 2007.

the use of multi-occupant business centres or regional offices for larger businesses. In other cases whole departments of government can be moved to regional centres. Such a concept would be eminently suitable for Ipswich as high-capacity broadband becomes available. Success of this model hinges on the ability to move large volumes of data, voice, and video between regional centres, suburbs, and cities. The richness of the experiences will increasingly be enhanced by higher end services such as 'in service' quality conferencing services and is directly linked to the quality and extent of the broadband services.[48]

The use of personal vehicles accounts for somewhere between 30-50 percent of greenhouse gas emissions. The major gain to the environment from telecommuting is the decrease in the number of automobile trips. Studies in many different countries demonstrate that savings for the environment from telework and telecommuting activity can be immense. Vast numbers of electronic documents are now generated daily that were once printed on paper. Newspaper circulation is declining in large part due to competition from electronic forms of news. These trends are likely to accelerate in the future.

Teleconferencing has similar implications. With ordinary bandwidth, teleconferencing has been a poor substitute for conference attendance for the last fifteen years. Now, long-distance, short-duration business travel can in the right circumstances be replaced with 'in person' high-quality online conferencing facilities that are significantly more efficient in terms of cost, time, energy, and emissions.

Aviation greenhouse emissions are rapidly increasing with increases in air travel. By 2020, emissions from aviation may have doubled since the protocol baseline year of 1990.[49] There is a clear disharmony between the rapid growth that has been witnessed in the aviation sector and the pressure for carbon reductions. The alternative to aviation travel for many aspects of business is high-definition, bandwidth-hungry video conferencing. Specific purpose, tele-presence facilities could be designed into the commercial centres of Ipswich.

eCommerce

The definition and evolution of eCommerce has been explained previously, with the emphasis on commercial benefits. ECommerce is also environmentally friendly. Compared to conventional shopping eCommerce has been found to generate 36 percent less conventional air pollutants, 23 percent less hazardous waste, and 9 percent less greenhouse gases.[50] ECommerce also reduces retail and warehouse space requirements,

---

[48]   Telstra Climate Risk Report: Towards a High-Bandwidth Low-Carbon Future, 2008.

[49]   Telstra Climate Risk Report: Towards a High-Bandwidth Low-Carbon Future, 2008.

[50]   Cited by Joseph Fuhr in the ACI Broadband Services Report, October 2007.

which in turn reduces energy requirements to build, heat, and cool such space. Another feature of eCommerce activity which does produce considerable environmental savings is the incidence of Internet-based research for products, services, prices, and location by potential buyers. This may lead to an online transaction or it may lead finally to a visit to a bricks-and-mortar establishment.

Online commercial behaviour also has significant implications for supply chain management. As traditional manufacturing and commercial companies put the supply chain online and reduce inventories, overproduction, unnecessary capital expenditures, paper transactions, and mistaken orders they achieve greater output with less energy consumption. Once again the effectiveness of this online activity will be determined by the quality and extent of the broadband services.

Substituting Bits for Atoms

This is referred to as dematerialisation in some quarters and means replacing high-carbon products and activities with low-carbon or no-carbon alternatives. Substituting face-to-face meetings with videoconferencing or paper with e-billing can play a significant role in reducing emissions. The trend towards the distribution and sale of music and DVDs online is similarly important in the entertainment world.

Like eCommerce, eGovernment could have a major impact on reducing emissions through the transformation of public service delivery. Many paper-based services can be moved into the digital environment. There are also major energy efficiencies to be achieved in the governmental supply chain. Although a credible start has been made on the implementation of eGovernment systems and services, the poor quality and limited extent of broadband infrastructure has been a retarding factor in the take up of this concept.

Intelligent Buildings and Smart Homes in Ipswich

The origins of Intelligent Buildings and Building Management Systems both have roots in the industrial sector in the 1970s, from the systems and controls used to automate production processes and to optimise plant performance. The concepts and applications were then adapted, developed, and modularised during the 1980s, enabling transferability of the technology to the residential and commercial markets. The next chapter in the life of intelligent buildings opens in a major way with the roll-out of high-capacity broadband infrastructure to provide for sophisticated networking and remote monitoring and management.

To capture the imagination of an increasingly digitally savvy world, Ipswich could incorporate state-of-the-art ICT infrastructure for intelligent buildings and smart homes. The essence of intelligent buildings lies in the control technologies, which allow integration, automation, and optimisation of all services and equipment. Later developments in commercial and residential applications were based on distributed intelligence microprocessors. The use of these technologies allows the optimisation of various site and building services, often yielding significant cost reductions. With increased awareness of energy use concerns, energy efficiency is fast becoming part of real estate and facilities management, and operations strategies. The concepts are now making rapid inroads into the domestic residential sector.

With the widespread adoption of digital technologies (and now high-capacity broadband) there has been a profound change within homes in respect of how people shop for goods and services, conduct business, manage resources, find entertainment, and maintain independence and autonomy as they enter old age. As the perception of banks, shops, universities, communities, and cities change in response to new technologies such as high-capacity broadband, homebuilding management systems are taking on a new importance.

Services and equipment that utilise these networks include security, home theatre and entertainment, telephones, door phones and intercoms, PCs and Internet networks, surveillance cameras, driveway vehicle sensors, communication thermostats, motorised blinds and curtains, entry systems, and irrigation systems.

An Intelligent Power Grid for the Western Corridor of South East Queensland

The development of an intelligent power grid would be an exciting possibility for the Western Corridor once high-capacity broadband is available. Any electricity grid is a collective of wires, transformers, and infrastructure that transports electricity from power plants to users. All conventional networks are huge inefficient grids that lose power in transmission and require an over capacity of generating capability to cope with unexpected demand. Most power networks without ubiquitous high-capacity bandwidth are blind and are unable to determine where their losses are incurred. Normally communication is one way only, from producer to consumer. In all but a few countries selling power back to the grid has not been enabled.

An intelligent grid has a minimal amount of waste and a highly efficient use of power. It is an electricity network that uses energy resources and advanced communication and control technologies to deliver electricity more cost effectively, with lower greenhouse intensity and in response to consumer needs.

Intelligent grids aim to achieve interactive energy generation and distribution, in which a proportion of the electricity generated by large conventional plants can be displaced by distributed generation from renewable energy sources, which include wind turbines, solar panels, micro turbines, fuel cells and co-generation. Such a system aims to generate energy closer to the point at which it is needed and seamlessly integrate intermittent renewable sources into the wider network.

If the quality and extent of broadband infrastructure is available to make the system run smarter, it is possible to reduce transmission losses, reduce wastage and make the overall supply itself greener.

Intelligent Transport Logistics

In a modern economy the physical transportation of goods has become a sector of massive importance (of even greater importance because of globalisation). The logistics of the transport industry involving packaging, transport, storage, consumer purchasing, and waste management are traditionally inefficient. Currently one third of the billions of kilometres travelled annually by Australian freight vehicles are without loads. Network-enabled vehicles and load monitoring systems that reduce unladen and under laden trips can now be created. Intelligent logistics comprising a range of ICTs have been developed that enable companies to monitor, optimise, and manage operations with a view to:

- reducing storage needed for inventory
- reducing fuel consumption
- reducing kilometres driven
- reducing the frequency of vehicles travelling empty or partially loaded

In Australia the road freight sector is responsible for 36 percent of the transport sector's emissions and 5 percent of the nation's total emissions.[51]

What is clearly needed for this industry is a real-time freight management system which goes far beyond typical in-house conventional freight management systems. Stepping up to such a system would involve mobile data networks to enable freight brokers to identify loads, vehicle locations, destinations, and load status in order to offer freight to empty or partially laden vehicles. The technology that is essential to make the system work includes broadband networks, messaging platforms, telematics, supply chain software, real-time route optimisation software, base management platforms, and forecasting and replenishment planning systems. The Western Corridor of South East Queensland is a major Australian transport hub. With ubiquitous high-capacity broadband available, the development of a major Queensland/NSW or even a national, real-time freight management system would be an intriguing possibility for Ipswich.

---

[51] Telstra Climate Risk Report: Towards a High-Bandwidth Low-Carbon Future, 2008.

Personalised Public Transport

Serious and reliable broadband networks provide the foundation for a public transport service on demand. Personalised public transport allows the user to order public transport provided by an integrated network of multi-occupant taxis, minibuses, buses, and trains which start at the front door. The objective of the PPT system is to exceed the efficiency of using the private car with faster speeds door to door, greater flexibility, and lower costs. Other opportunities have been identified with the potential for web-based intelligence to increase car pooling and therefore the net efficiency of car use.

The net effect of personalised public transport is:

- increased flexibility for the customer
- reduced waiting times for the customer
- increasing the use of public transport within the catchment
- more frequent services
- higher speed arterial services
- increased commercial viability of all transport suppliers

Many of the tools employed to tackle major environmental challenges in today's world are information and communications-based products and services. Sophisticated computing systems are at the forefront. Communication networks have, however, since the advent of broadband added serious value to the work of computers. Extra-ordinary developments in the capabilities of communications technology has in effect been a 'quiet revolution'.

Together, computing and communications technologies enable a wide range of other technologies to address air and water pollution, understand global warming and aquatic ecosystems, facilitate recycling and achieve more efficient use of energy. The planet's response to climate change already is, and will, well into the future, involve highly sophisticated communication networks and super computing power. High-capacity broadband infrastructure is vital at the global, national, regional and local level.

Intelligent Transport Systems

The introduction of intelligent transport systems where vehicles communicate with their surroundings including other vehicles is expected to be widespread within the next ten years. ITS provide the opportunity for more efficient use of road infrastructure and energy. Cars can be managed to optimise road speed to suit conditions, traffic lights and pedestrian crossings. Electric vehicles can be managed to optimise use of charging stations.

The Social Impact of High-capacity Broadband

The impact of high-capacity broadband on the lifestyle of families and individuals, young and old, in Ipswich will be considerable. Since the general public gained access to the Internet in 1993-4, firstly by narrowband dial-up access and since 1998 by very ordinary, so-called broadband speeds (generally less than 1 Mbps), a social and cultural revolution has been underway.

In the last fifteen years, individuals, families, and communities have experienced quite extraordinary changes in respect of how, when, and where they live, work, and play.

With access to high-capacity broadband, in the next fifteen years the same individuals, families, and communities will experience a paradigm shift in terms of the way they communicate, live their lives, earn their living, enjoy their retirement, access services, and select their entertainment.

Fixed-line applications at home, at the workplace, and in community facilities, and ubiquitous mobile devices handling speeds of more than 50 Mbps will usher in a new era of collaboration and interaction based on real-time, high-resolution, and ultimately 3D interactive services.

Everyone with access will benefit from a range of very fundamental choices including:

- the option of no longer having to do many time-consuming and, possibly, boring tasks
- being able to do many selected traditional tasks faster, more effectively and at more convenient times
- choosing from a kaleidoscope of enriched new functions and activities

Most of the enhanced existing services and new services will involve lifestyle benefits for individuals and families, and benefits associated with the delivery of community services.

Home Based Entertainment—Enriched Options for the Residents of Ipswich

Whilst the business world and government agencies will comprise a very important part of the demand for next-generation systems, the real breadth and depth of the demand for high-capacity broadband will come from home users.

Technology from radio and record players to television and DVDs has a long history of opening up new forms of entertainment. However, it is the broadband revolution that is now

125

defining exciting possibilities to improve, expand, and enhance recreational and entertainment experiences. The availability of high-capacity broadband is redefining consumers' relationships with traditional media and pointing the way to a more entertaining future by improving the quality of entertainment, offering more choices in entertainment, allowing more control of the media and enabling consumers to participate in creating media.

Demand for consistent and higher speeds and higher upstream capacity is growing as new Web services and the uploading and downloading of video in particular increase in usage. To put the time frames in perspective, Flickr photo sharing was launched in 2004, YouTube video sharing in 2005, Facebook in September 2006, Gmail in 2007, BBC iPlayer in December 2007, and Apple TV 'Take Two' in January 2008. The consequent growth in traffic over the last few years has been dramatic. YouTube for example currently consumes as much bandwidth as the entire Internet required in 2000.[52]

In early 2008, Cisco forecast 42 percent annual growth to at least 2011 for global Internet consumer traffic.[53] Perhaps the most challenging aspect of the growth in demand for increased bandwidth from the home will be simultaneous use of bandwidth-hungry applications such as home-based business operation, videoconferencing, real-time online gaming, distance education experiences, social networking, and remote health monitoring.

eHealth and Telemedicine in Ipswich

Health care systems all over Australia are under great and increasing pressure associated with escalating costs, changing disease patterns, the ageing of the population, and increasing mobility of patients and professionals. The power of information and particularly communications technologies have been harnessed in creative ways in recent years as health care professionals and administrators strive to deliver better and more efficient health care services.

Many future improvements in health care will originate not from better drugs or better doctors but from better-managed information. Some experts in the field believe the world is on the cusp of a paradigm shift in the nature of managing and delivering health care services because of the potential of next-generation networks.

In practical terms, the concepts of eHealth and telemedicine basically date from the late 1990s.

---

[52] Report on Next Generation Broadband for the Broadband Stakeholder Group: by Plum Consulting. London. June 2008.

[53] 'The Exabyte Era' (an exabyte is a billion gigabytes), Cisco, 14 January 2008.

In the Journal of Medical Internet Research,[54] G. Eysenbach defined eHealth as long ago as 2001 as

> '. . . *an emerging field at the intersection of informatics, public health, and business, referring to health services and information delivered or enhanced through Internet and related technologies* . . .'

In most instances, eHealth features networked services such as electronic messaging between hospitals and other health care participants for communication of clinical and administrative data and telemedicine such as telepathology services and teleconsultations. Broadband deployment has led to quite revolutionary developments in telemedicine, especially in respect of the ability to make diagnoses and provide treatment for patients via high-speed two-way voices, data and video transmission.

The principal areas of health care in which access to broadband has made a significant difference include:

- reduced health care costs
- increased access to health information
- improved quality of health care
- superior access to health care
- greater prevention of illness
- a shift from hospital care to primary and home care
- providing better citizen centred health care

Access to high-capacity broadband will produce even greater strides and achievements in these areas. eHealth services can be a valuable complement to the existing high-quality health services available in Ipswich city.

Education Services in Ipswich

In the foreseeable future, fibre to the classroom and, quite conceivably, fibre to the desk will be expected as a key feature of contemporary education facilities. High-speed wireless systems could also be part of the mix.

Education systems are confronting challenges not altogether dissimilar to their counterparts in the health service, especially with regard to escalating costs. As in health, the power of information and communications technologies has been harnessed in creative ways in recent years to assist education professionals and administrators to

---

[54]   Volume 3 of 2001.

deliver better education services. The availability of greater and more reliable bandwidth since the late 1990s has had a major impact.

Distance education is perhaps the most obvious but certainly not the only educational use of bigger pipes.

With a large proportion of post-secondary students living off campus, there is an ever increasing need for extra bandwidth to ensure that such students receive the same quality of educational experience as students on campus. Many smaller regional campuses are turning to high-capacity broadband to enable them to provide their students with the same quality of instruction as larger institutions.

Education for the young and the not so young is no longer confined to sitting in a classroom and taking notes (chalk and talk). Increasingly, the learning journey at all levels of education involves Internet-based research, online collaboration with fellow students, videoconferences with remotely based experts and celebrities and real-time video-based exploration.[55]

In other aspects of education the following changes can be found:

- high quality video is providing meaningful two-way, interactive, real time learning experiences
- education and gaming technologies are beginning to merge into learning based simulations that are demanding massive bandwidth
- parents are able to use the Internet to monitor their children's academic progress
- companies are using sophisticated online technologies to save on workforce development costs

Ultimately, our ability to expand access to education and cater for multiple learning styles depends on the extent and quality of the broadband infrastructure.

eGovernment Service Delivery

Part of the foundation of any successful community is its system of government and community services, which involve the collection and dissemination of information. eGovernment service delivery was one of the clearly articulated objectives of Global Info-Links in 1993. Successful communities also have strong bonds between their members and with other communities.

---

[55]   Atkinson and Castro: Digital Quality of Life (ITIF), Washington, October 2008.

Effective and reliable telecommunications infrastructure has made possible a new era of online communities which are a valuable complement to traditional geographical communities. Online systems and services now make it possible for citizens of smaller and remote communities to have access to products and cultural opportunities that were previously only available in large cities. In recent years, communities of interest have become very important to people irrespective of whether they live in urban, suburban, rural, or remote locations.

Because ICTs (especially broadband infrastructure) facilitate the collection, analysis, and distribution of information, the technology is central to the functioning of all community agencies irrespective of size or location.

Government departments and community agencies have been prime beneficiaries of the major breakthroughs in the provision of broadband services in a number of ways that include the following:

- the transformation of complicated legacy systems into customer-friendly systems
- making government more efficient
- the provision of data required for various forms of problem solving
- promoting government transparency and accountability
- the provision of 'access' to important data outside business hours
- reducing the costs of service delivery

In our increasingly complex world, the sophistication of the data that can be reliably transmitted by government and community agencies to people depends on the extent and quality of the broadband infrastructure.

Personal Security and Public Safety in Ipswich

During the last twenty years, there has seen a major shift in concern about personal security and public safety. The level of concern does vary significantly, however, from place to place. In Ipswich, as in most other Australian communities, there is a generally increased demand for state-of-the-art technological responses to and solutions for personal security and public safety. In the 1990s Ipswich was a world leader in the development of closed-circuit TV technology with its Ipswich Safe City program.

Householders and individuals are increasingly turning to sophisticated ICTs to:

- secure homes from crime and other hazards
- make vehicles safer

- reduce auto theft
- prevent accidents
- respond to emergencies

It is hard to overstate the importance of broadband technology in ensuring public safety. Fast, interactive, content-rich services that are the fundamentals of high-capacity broadband in times of emergencies are now relied upon to simultaneously deliver voice, high-speed data, and high-quality video for a range of strategies. Beyond local emergencies, at a national or regional level, broadband infrastructure is essential for real-time interagency coordination, monitoring, and mobilisation. Ultimately, it makes good sense to develop the infrastructure in a way that features multiple carriers, disaster backup services, multiple facilities, and decentralisation. Top quality broadband infrastructure has made a significant difference in a range of key activities designed to protect public safety. They include the following:

- the use of biometric screening
- enhancing remote surveillance
- better understanding of complex weather systems
- replacing traditional mail services with electronic mail services
- facilitating remote working stations (telework)
- transferring large data and image files at high speed
- facilitating the involvement of mobile robots in hazardous situations
- providing accurate information for offsite managers dealing with emergencies

The effectiveness of public safety strategies always rely heavily upon having the right information delivered to the right people at the right time. A large range of sophisticated ICT products and services can now be made available via broadband infrastructure to more effectively manage responses to natural disasters and national emergencies.

PART 5

CONCLUSION

• Why It Happened in Ipswich in 1992-7?
• A Contribution to the Transformation of a City

Why did it happen in Ipswich in 1992-7?

> '. . . A dream with courage is innovation,
>   a dream without courage is a delusion . . .'
>
> **Milan Kundera**

When we launched Global Info-Links, we speculated that in years to come, people would undoubtedly ask, 'Why did it happen in Ipswich?'

The answer is, of course, the convergence of a whole series of classic ingredients that are always to be found where a first-class innovation occurs namely:

- the imagination and the vision
- the courage
- the champions of the concept
- access to adequate financial resources
- a keen sense of timing
- the fundamental support infrastructure
- but, above all, commitment of a dedicated team to drive the idea through to completion (hard work)

In Ipswich during 1992-7 we had the lot.

The imagination and the vision at the top came from three quite different teams of councillors—1991-4, 1994-5 and 1995-9[56]—and a CEO who fervently believed in the future of his city, Jamie Quinn. Commitment to the city's future at this level ensured that the necessary financial resources were made available.

---

[56]   See attachments.

Our sense of timing was fortunate indeed. Five years before 1992 the project would have been before its time. Five years after 1992 and we would have been 'also-rans'. In fact, we were ready for business at a time when the demand for services on the information highways of the world was exploding.

The commitment of the project team and their back-up staff to drive the project through to completion surpasses anything I've seen anywhere in my professional career.

Our initial project team in 1993 was an interesting combination to tackle a major economic and social development initiative and involved the corporate manager of development investment, the corporate manager of research and development, the corporate manager of information systems, the city librarian, and the CEO. We added six other key members to the team as the project unfolded: a computer marketing specialist and development manager, a technical services manager, a systems services librarian, the geographic information systems manager, and two administrative support staff. It was my privilege to be chairman of that project team. Not only did these people deliver a very high quality of input, they were tremendous with their sense of humour and charitable in their responses to some of the strangest and most unusual requests for help.

Many of our key people, at various levels, sacrificed a great deal of family life over twenty-four months. Within the Ipswich City Council, no fewer than fifty or sixty people had hands-on involvement at various stages of the project.

External friends and allies, of course, contributed in a very substantial way.

Sometimes it was specific technical advice that we needed; other times it was simply reassurance that what we were doing was possible and that we weren't really crazy.

In this respect, we were indebted to the Centre for Information Technology Research at the University of Queensland, Interactive Presentations, the Australian Centre for Innovation and International Competitiveness, Data 3, Datamaster, JTech, Telecom, our friends at the Wellington City Council, our local Education Advisory Group, the Information Industries Board, DEET, DBIRB, Arthur Advertising, the legal firm of Fez Ruthning, the Department of Social Security who had assisted us to pilot the Seniors Project, the education department of Queensland, the Queensland government's library board, librarians at no fewer than a dozen university and state libraries, the staff of AARNet, the Prentice Centre, and the men and women who designed and constructed the building. [57]Lindy McKeown, Poppy Masselos, and Dr Hilda des Arts were three special local individuals without whom the education module and the SeniorNet could never have been built.

---

[57]   The architects were John Simpson and Associates of Brisbane, Queensland.

After 1997, the outstanding effort involved in managing the long haul was provided by Neil McPhillips, Peter Gillard, and Darryl Cross.

In essence, it all happened in 1992-7 because at that time the Ipswich City Council had the vision, the courage of its convictions, and the talent. The city's leaders had watched the once mighty industrial economy of the city decline and were determined to embark upon an economic turnaround strategy involving a series of fundamentally new directions. The council decided it was time for intervention in a powerfully proactive way to guide the economic and community development of the city.

A Contribution to the Transformation of a City

> '... Ipswich was a great innovator and builder in its early history. The success of Ipswich's courageous and early entry into the new age of information and communications created community confidence to again positively embrace change and growth. This community confidence empowered its elected council to lead Ipswich out of an era of minimal growth, high unemployment, and high crime rates ...'
>
> Jamie Quinn, former CEO of the City of Ipswich
> (Deputy CEO, 1984-9; CEO, 1989-2006)
> 12 September 2008

In 1992, when we set about the task of creating Ipswich as an online community our objective was to harness the power of the Internet to create an information-rich community. It seems we did that and a little more.

The city of Ipswich has undergone a remarkable period of transformation in the last eighteen years, 1992-2010. Whilst outstanding leadership has been provided throughout by the Ipswich City Council, highly significant inputs have been made by the Queensland State Government, the Australian Federal Government, and the private sector. The early years, 1992-7, constituted a classic turnaround and take-off period. Post 1997 has been a story of serious transformation. A measure of that transformation is to be found in a range of data as presented below:

- In 1992, unemployment in Ipswich was nudging 13 percent, including 25 percent of youth under twenty-five years of age. By 2006 unemployment was down to 5.9 percent; in January 2010 it stood as low as 5.3 percent.
- Between 2002 and 2009, the unimproved capital land value for Ipswich increased massively from $2.2 billion to $10.7 billion.
- The population of Ipswich increased by 9.7 percent over three years to 2006 and grew at the rate of 4.1 percent in 2007-8 and 3.8 percent in 2008-9. Latest Queensland Government 'medium series' estimates forecast that Ipswich's population will grow from 160,000 in 2009 to 434,000 in 2031, representing an

average annual growth of 4.6 percent for the twenty-two years up to 2031. This is the highest projected growth of all ten SEQ local governments and outstrips the aggregate SEQ-projected average annual growth of 1.8 percent.
- Building approval value increased by 289 percent over three years to 2006.
- The number of businesses increased by 16 percent over three years to 2006.
- The number of taxable individuals increased by 15 percent in the three years to 2005.

The key components of the turnaround and take-off period, 1992-7, included the following:

- restructure and revival of the city council's finances in the period 1987 to 1993
- a fundamental restructure of the administration and operations of the Ipswich City Council in 1992
- the IT-led economic development strategy, *Global Info-Links,* that established Ipswich as Australia's first online community 1993-5
- the construction of Ipswich Global Information Centre as a world-class library service, 1994
- the campaign (1993-6), the actual decision (1996), and eventual establishment (1999) of a university campus in Ipswich
- the amalgamation of the two local governing authorities, Ipswich City Council and Moreton Shire Council in 1995
- acceleration of the Springfield development from 1995, as one of Australia's largest master planned communities with an ultimate population of 85,000 people
- the commitment by the Ipswich City Council and the Queensland State Government to re-develop the Ipswich Railway Workshops, 1994-5

The hallmarks of the city's quite remarkable transformation since 1997 include a wide range of infrastructure and planning initiatives that include the following:

- the decision by the Australian Federal Government to transform the Amberley air Force base into Australia's largest integrated defence facility
- major expansion of the capacity of the Carole Park Industrial Estate, Synergy Park, and Citiswich Business Park
- the development of the Railway Workshop Museum in North Ipswich
- the release in 2005 of the 'Ipswich 2020 and Beyond' master plan for the city which focuses on three major activity centres, various smaller designated centres, and other major industrial and business job generators
- the release of the South East Queensland Regional Plan
- the release of the Ipswich Regional Centre Strategy

- the establishment of a campus of the University of Southern Queensland at Springfield
- the establishment of the Riverlink Shopping Centre in Ipswich Central on the Bremer River north bank
- creation of Ipswich River Heart Parklands in Ipswich Central on the Bremer River south bank
- the establishment of Orion Shopping Centre, including downtown Main Street in Springfield Central as the core of the Springfield Town Centre
- assured water security through access to the SEQ Water Grid, including the $800 Million Southern Regional Water Pipeline running through Ipswich's major industrial corridor and the $2.3 Billon Western Corridor Recycled Water Scheme at Bundamba which is the southern hemisphere's largest purified recycled water scheme
- the $366 million Centenary Highway extension through Ripley Valley to the Cunningham Highway
- the development of the Polaris Data Centre at Springfield Central
- the release of the Ipswich City Council Economic Development plan for 2009-31

Developments which have been announced and which are either underway or in the advanced planning stage include the following:

- a $4 billion upgrade of the Ipswich Motorway connecting Brisbane and Ipswich
- the Ipswich Central City redevelopment
- the Aerospace and Defence Support Centre at Amberley
- the establishment of the Ipswich InfoCity initiative
- a rail loop from Darra (on Brisbane/Ipswich line) through Springfield and Ripley Valley to Ipswich Central—the $837 million Darra to Springfield section is currently under construction with the remaining Springfield to Ipswich corridor identified (estimated construction cost of $2.3 billion)
- the Ripley Valley master planned community to accommodate 120,000 people
- development of the Swanbank Enterprise Park, Redbank River Park, Wulkuaka/ Karribin Industrial Estate, and Ebenezer Industrial Park
- the Queensland Government's decentralisation policy and the decision to relocate the following HQ offices to Ipswich
  - Queensland Rail
  - SEQ Water Grid Manager
  - Seqwater (dams and treatment)
  - WaterSecure (manufactured water)
  - LinkWater (bulk water transport)

In 2007, Ipswich was recognised in the International Awards for Livable Communities as the World's Most Livable City with a population between 75,000 and 200,000. The LivCom Awards which are endorsed by the United Nations Environment Program were launched in 1997 and are the world's only awards competition focusing on best practice regarding the management of the local environment. LivCom is non-political, embracing all nations and cultures, and over fifty countries are represented within the awards.

In the words of the people interviewed for this book, the online community concept and the Global Info-Links project acted as a catalyst that led to an explosion of ideas and thoughts, introduced Ipswich to the information highways of the world, revolutionised the way the people of Ipswich accessed information, was the basis of a major shift in the psyche of the community, turned around the internal and external perception of Ipswich, provided the key to a highly competitive structure for telecommunications services in Ipswich, established for the first time a connection between the library service and information technology, placed Ipswich at the forefront of a technological revolution, created a very important early chapter in the evolution of eCommerce in Australia, changed what was a strictly blue-collar community impression of Ipswich and provided the magnet which ultimately attracted the University of Queensland to establish a campus in Ipswich, and created a community confidence which empowered the elected council to lead Ipswich out of its decline.

Global Info-Links was a key part of a fairly revolutionary IT-led economic development strategy. The IT-led economic strategy was just one important part of an economic turnaround strategy for the city. What started life as Australia's first community-owned ISP, Global Info-Links, in 1994, is today comfortably embedded in the South East Queensland Community Telecommunications Company. In 1992,[58] the Internet was virtually unheard of in Australia and most parts of the world. At the end of the first decade of the twenty-first century the Internet is ubiquitous and taken for granted. Today, tens of thousands of homes and many thousands of businesses in Ipswich use the technology that has transformed the way we work, take our leisure, access information, and basically organise our life. In many respects that transformation began in Australia in a strategic way in Ipswich.

---

[58] But for a small handful of researchers, military strategists, and technical specialists.

PART 6

THE TIMELINE

A Timeline for Australia's First Online Community

1991

- Tim Berners-Lee and Robert Cailliau develop the basic technology for the World Wide Web in Switzerland.

1992

- Ipswich City Council undertakes a major review of its management structure and priorities.
- The world's first web pages were published.
- Ipswich City Council appoints an Economic Development Committee for the first time.
- The Ipswich Development Investment Group was established to develop and implement the Ipswich City Council's economic development program.
- 8 December—First meeting convened by IDI Group to discuss a strategy to achieve a university in Ipswich.
- 10 December—Memorandum from the IDIM to the general manager of Ipswich City Council, recommending the development of a new library and information service for the city of Ipswich.
- 10 December—Memorandum from IDIM to the Mayor of Ipswich City Council, recommending the formation of a taskforce to establish a university in Ipswich.

1993

- 12 January—First demonstration of the Internet in Ipswich, organised by the IDI Group and CiTR (University of Queensland) for all Aldermen and senior staff.
- January to May—Ipswich City Council evaluated available online information services such as Dialogue, ILANET, AussieNet, and the Internet. Decision was made to use the Internet for global connectivity.
- Ipswich City Council adopted its first Economic Development Program.

- 5 February—First meeting of the university taskforce held at Ipswich City Council.
- 24 May—Concept outline for 'Ipswich Information Links' incorporating an ISP and a new library presented to council by Ipswich Development Investment Manager.
- 24 June—Ipswich City Council agreed to proceed with 'Ipswich Info Links' program. Initial project team appointed comprising Ipswich development investment manager as chairman, R & D manager, information systems manager, city librarian, and the general manager.
- 28 June—First official connection to the Internet by the Ipswich City Council.
- July—Ipswich City Council applied for and received affiliate membership of the AARNet network (which supplied the Internet to Australian universities)
- Mosaic—the first user-friendly graphic interface to the Internet was released.
- October—Ipswich City Council and the Centre for Information Technology Research (University of Queensland) sign an MOU to develop a Technical Framework Study for the Ipswich Info-Links initiative.
- October—Ipswich City Council decides to build a new library building to house the 'Ipswich Info-Links Service' and the traditional library services.
- 10 November—Ipswich University Taskforce presents the Ipswich case to the University of Queensland for a university campus to be established in the city.

1994

- Technical Framework Study for Ipswich Info-Links completed by CiTR.
- Ipswich City Council renames its online initiative 'Ipswich Global Info-Links'.
- 8 December—The first 100 households in Ipswich were connected to the Internet via Global Info-Links.
- 8 December—Australia's first community Web site (Ipswich) released.
- 8 December—All 121 schools in the city of Ipswich became the first schools in Australia to be connected to the Internet, as part of the education module of GIL.
- 8 December—Ipswich City Council became the first local authority in Australia and one of the first in the world to deliver information to ratepayers and households online.

1995

- 3 February—The Ipswich Global Information Centre Building and the new information service was officially launched by former Federal Minister for Science and Technology, Hon Barry Jones, MHR, and former Mayor of Ipswich, Mr Dave Underwood.
- 13 February—Australia's first SeniorNet launched in Ipswich.

- 28 March—Ipswich City Council and Moreton Shire Council officially merged into the city of Ipswich.
- Ipswich launched Australia's first community driven eCommerce program.
- March—Education Advisory Group formed by GIL management team.
- July—Australian Vice-Chancellors' Committee sold all non-university customers for the Internet to Telstra.
- September—Ipswich City Council became the first local authority in Australia to invite tenders for the supply of products and services via the Internet.

1996

- The Australian Federal Government rejected the Ipswich City Council's application for funding ($2.5Million) to hard-wire the CBD of Ipswich.
- 10 December—University of Queensland announced its intention to establish a campus in Ipswich.
- 11 December—University of Queensland Vice-Chancellor, Professor John Hay, states in the Queensland Times '. . . *That Global Info-Links was a major factor in the decision to come to Ipswich and in the design of courses to be offered at the new campus . . .*'

1997

- February—University taskforce wound up and replaced by UQ Ipswich Support Group.
- Annual Revenue for GIL exceeded $2 million.
- Global Info-Links was operating more than 400 modems.
- Modem speeds for Internet connections reached 33.3 Kbps.
- GIL subscriber base reaches 7,500.

1998

- Global Info-Links as an Ipswich City Council-owned and operated ISP was established as a commercial business unit within Ipswich City Council.
- The volume of data exceeds the volume of voice traffic on Australia's telecommunications infrastructure for the first time.
- June—Friends of UQ Ipswich established.
- August—GIL had more than 10,000 registered subscribers, 4,000 business clients, and hosted 350 business web sites
- October—GIL help desk handling 800 calls per week.

1999

- 22 June—UQ Ipswich was formally opened.
- Global Info-Links was physically relocated to North Ipswich as part of the re-development of the Ipswich Railway Workshops.

2000

- February/March—First intake of students at UQ Ipswich
- Australia registers its 600th Internet Service Provider.
- GIL achieves 15,000 subscribers.
- Global Info-Links Pty Ltd (with the Ipswich City Council as the sole shareholder) was established.

2001

- September—Global Info-Links Pty Ltd formally became part of the community telco iTEL, which is an unlisted public company. iTEL was subsequently renamed South East Queensland Community Telco in 2008.

PART 7

REFERENCES

References

Publications and reports used in the production of this book include the following:

Atkinson and Castro: 'Digital Quality of Life', ITIF, Washington, October 2008.

Atkinson and McKay: 'Digital Prosperity', IT and Innovation Foundation, March 2007.

Australian Bureau of Statistics: A Demographic Overview of Ipswich, 1994.

Robert Bell: 'Broadband Economies', I.C.F., New York, 2009.

M Bryce: 'Building Online Communities', Presentation to the Wheatbelt Development Commission of WA, June 2008.

M Bryce: 'Harnessing the Knowledge Economy', Keynote address to the Connecting Up Conference, Adelaide, May 2004

M Bryce: 'Kick-starting the Online Community', Presentation, 1998.

M Bryce: 'IT&T Implications for Regional Development', Griffith University, 1998.

Roger Clarke: 'Origins and Nature of the Internet in Australia', Xamax Consulting Pty Ltd, 2004.

D'Costa and Kelly: 'Broadband as a Platform for development', OECD Conference, November 2008

Joseph Fuhr: 'Broadband Services Report', American Consumer Institute, October 2007.

P Gillard: 'The Internet: A New Marketing Tool', Presentation to the Australian Marketing Institute, November 1997.

P Gillard: 'Internet-Web of the Future', Australian Mining Conference, October 1995.

P Gillard and Cathy Watson: 'Libraries—The Next Generation', Presentation to the Public Librarians Annual Conference, May 1997.

Global Info-Links Web Committee: Minutes of the meeting to approve first Ipswich web site, Ipswich City Council, 8 November 1994.

Global Info-Links Information Guide: 'Ipswich Australia Smart City', Ipswich City Council, 1995.

Global Info-Links: Publication by Ipswich City Council, 1996.

Samuel Hinton: 'Towards a Critical Theory of the Internet', PhD Thesis, La Trobe University, November 2005.

Walt Howe: 'A Brief History of the Internet', Walt Howes Internet Learning Centre, 2007.

Professor Sid Huff: *Wired Wellington-InfoCity Project*, Victoria University, Wellington, May 1996.

Ipswich City Council: 'The Case for a University in Ipswich', Presentation by the Ipswich University Taskforce, November 1993.

Ipswich City Council: 'Memorandum from IDIM to Mayor Re University for Ipswich', 10 December 1992. Ref G14-01 (12012100)

Significant Bits Journal: 'Ipswich City Council Presents Global Info-Links', Vol 10, No. 1, December 1994.

Ipswich City Council: 'Ipswich 2010—Economic Development, Building on our Strengths', August 1995.

Ipswich City Council: 'Global Info-Links—Your Expressway to the World', 1995.

Ipswich City Council: 'Impact of the Internet on Local Government', Presentation, 1999.

Ipswich City Council: 'Economic Development Plan for Ipswich City', 2009-31.

Ipswich City Council: 'Ipswich Library and Information Services—Coping with Growth', 2008-26.

ITU: 'World Telecommunications Indicators Database', 2008.

Dr Wendell Joice: 'Evolution of Telework in the Federal Government', US Office of General Services, 2000.

L. Kleinrock: *The Rules of Engagement—Then and Now,* Computer Science Department, UCLA, February 2004.

Judith Nissen: *The Road to UQ Ipswich*, University of Queensland, 2004.

Richard Naylor: 'Multimedia and Interactive Technology at Wellington City Council', Presentation, May 1995.

'An Oral History of the Internet: How the Web was Won', Vanity Fair, July 2008.

Carlota Perez: *Technological Revolutions and Financial Capital*, Edward Elgar, UK, 2005.

P Pisasale: 'Online Service Delivery in the Ipswich Region', Presentation at Ipswich City Council, 1998.

William H Read & Jan L Youtie: *Telecommunications Strategy for Economic Development*, Preagar, London, 1996.

Report of the Asian Productivity Organisation: Basic Research on Information Technology. Nordica International Ltd, 1990.

Report of the Broadband Stakeholders Group: June 2008.

Zik Saleeba: 'Network Access in Australia', Monash University, 1994.

SeniorNet Association Incorporated: 'Eleventh Annual Report', June 2007.

Wes Tatters: 'Global Info-Links Internet Australasia', May 1995.

TAT Cables Report: 'World Telecommunications Development.' 1997.

Telstra Climate Risk Report: 'Towards a High-Bandwidth Low-Carbon Future', 2008.

Kevin Wright & Dr Hilda Des Arts: 'A Guide to Establishing a SeniorNet Branch in your District', SeniorNet Association, 1996.

Peter Young: 'Granny Retires to a Computing Future', Sunday Mail, 12 February 1995.

PART 8

APPENDICES

Appendix 1

ACRONYMS AND CERTAIN SPECIFIC TERMS

AARNET	Australian Academic and Research Network
ABS	Australian Bureau of Statistics
APO	Asian Productivity Organisation
AVCC	Australian Vice-Chancellors' Committee
B2B	Business to Business (eCommerce term)
B2C	Business to Consumer (eCommerce term)
C2B	Consumer to Business (eCommerce term)
C2C	Consumer to Consumer (eCommerce term)
CERN	One of the world's largest physics laboratories in Switzerland
CiTR	Centre for Information Technology Research
CBD	Central Business District
ARPA	Advanced Research Projects Agency (USA)
DPI	Department of Primary Industry
DSL	Digital Subscriber Line
EDI	Electronic Data Interchange
FTTP	Fibre to the Premises
GEM	Global Electronic Market
ICC	Ipswich City Council
ICT	Information and Communications Technologies
IDIM	Ipswich Development Investment Manager (Ipswich City Council)
IDIG	Ipswich Development Investment Group
IRDC	Ipswich Region Development Corporation
IP	Internet Protocol
ITS	Intelligent Transport System

IT&T	Information Technology and Telecommunications
ISP	Internet Service Provider
iTEL	Ipswich Telecommunications Company
MHR	Member of the House of Representatives (Australian Parliament)
MOSAIC	The world's first graphical user-friendly interface for the Internet
SEQ	South East Queensland
SMEs	Small- and Medium-Sized Enterprises
SPRU	Science and Technology Policy Research Unit (UK)
TAFE	Technical and Further Education (Australia)
TCP	Transmission Control Protocol
VPN	Virtual Private Network

Appendix 2

THE ORIGINAL GLOBAL INFO-LINKS PROJECT TEAM

APPOINTED 24 JUNE 1993

Source: Global Info-Links electronic records 1994

Mal Bryce
AO, BA., Hon D Tech, FAICD

Aged fifty-one. Born in Bunbury, Western Australia. Mal is a former cabinet minister, company director, and management consultant. He has been heavily involved in the development of the IT&T sector of the Australian economy since the late 1970s. During the 1980s he pioneered the development of Australia's most successful Technology Park at Bentley in Western Australia, and has held directorship of six Australian science-based and IT companies since 1988. He is a former member of the

Prime Minister's Science and Engineering Council and numerous other IT industry advisory groups.

Mal was appointed as Corporate Manager of Development Investment with Ipswich City Council in December 1992 to design and implement the city's Economic Development Program. In that position he is Chairman of the GIL project team.

Neil McPhillips

Aged thirty-seven. Born in Toowoomba, Queensland. Neil has eighteen years local government experience ranging from finance and computing through to organisation management. Neil was appointed Corporate Manager of Research and Development with Ipswich City Council in March 1992. His knowledge and experience of local government has assisted the council to become recognised as a leader in its field. Neil's research and development expertise and innovative ability adds a further dimension to the skills base of the team of Global Info-Links.

Jamie Quinn
LGC, AIMM

Aged forty-one. Born in Ipswich, Queensland. Jamie is the Chief Executive Officer of Ipswich City Council. The council services a population of 78,000, employs 700 staff, operates a $70 M net budget and manages assets worth over $100 M. Jamie has extensive experience in local government management. He has held positions of Chief and Deputy Chief Executive Officer since 1974 in a diverse range of local governments throughout Queensland.

Jamie has specialist expertise in local government finances and was the architect of the financial restructure of the city of Ipswich which dramatically reduced the city's debt to equity ratio.

Roger Birch
B.Sc.

Aged forty-seven. Born in Manchester, United Kingdom. Roger has worked in most facets of the information technology field over the past twenty-six years, covering both government and private enterprise as well as computer supplier and user areas.

Most of this work has been in the development or control of technical areas, but has concentrated for the past ten to fifteen years on the use of advanced technology to provide service to users coupled with the delivery of those services to where people want them.

He joined Ipswich City Council in September 1992 as Information Systems Manager, and his role was expanded in January 1993 to include the City Library.

Roger Coleman
BA, Grad. Dip. Lib., AALIA

Aged forty-three. Born in Wellington, New Zealand.

Roger was appointed to the position of City Librarian in October 1992 and has played a key role in the design and construction of the *Ipswich Global Information Centre* as the hub of the Global Info-Links project.

Roger has an ongoing commitment to multicultural service initiatives. He has previously held senior positions within the Victorian public library system, most recently at Northcote and has had extensive background in innovative service development in socially and culturally diverse inner-urban environments.

Member of ACLIS (Queensland) Advocacy Sub-Committee. Has written articles for Incite and other professional journals, and contributed to the production of teaching resource materials in the areas of literacy, social education and the role of public libraries in resourcing these and other curriculum developments. Former member of the Management Committee of the University of Melbourne's Library and Information Management Alumni Association and Executive Member of the Victorian Community Information Network, a state-wide peak body for community information providers.

Appendix 3

Councillors of the City of Ipswich 1991-2012[59]

1991-1994

Underwood, David Francis—Mayor

Conway, Georgette Phyllis

Dwyer, Philip Kevin

Evans, Kathryn

Hanly, Denise

Kinnane, John William

Kruger, Norman Henry

McDonnell, Wayne N

Molloy, Graham Thomas

Pisasale, Paul John

Tully, Paul Gregory

1994-1995

Underwood, David Francis—Mayor

Conway, Georgette Phyllis

Gluyas, Richard D

Hanson, Pauline

Hope, Peter John

Hutchison, Graham D

Pender, Gerard P

Ranizowski, John

---

[59]   Prior to 1995, a councillor of Ipswich City Council was referred to as an 'Alderman'.

Tanner, A Raymond
Tully, Paul Gregory
Wykes, Susan. F

1995-2000
Nugent, Owen John—Mayor
Bloom, Francesca
Claridge, Christine
Gluyas, Richard D
Hanly, Denise
Hayes, Patricia (April 1995-February 1998)
Kalamafoni, Alf (April 1995-May 1998)
Nardi, Trevor (Appt. July 1998)
Pahlke, David Allen
Pender, Gerard P
Pisasale, Charles
Pisasale, Paul John
Russell, Neil (April 1998-March 2000)
Tully, Paul Gregory
Woods, Joan

2000-2004
Nugent, Owen John—Mayor
Antoniolli, Andrew
Attwood, Victor
Hanly, Denise
Morrison, David
Morrow, Heather
Nardi, Trevor
Pahlke, David Allen
Pisasale, Charles
Pisasale, Paul John
Tully, Paul Gregory

2004-2008
Pisasale, Paul John—Mayor
Antoniolli, Andrew
Attwood, Victor
Bromage, Cheryl
Ireland, Sheila
Morrison, David
Morrow, Heather

Nardi, Trevor
Pahlke, David Allen
Pisasale, Charles
Tully, Paul Gregory

2008-2012
Pisasale, Paul John—Mayor
Antoniolli, Andrew
Attwood, Victor
Bromage, Cheryl
Ireland, Sheila
Morrison, David
Morrow, Heather
Nardi, Trevor
Pahlke, David Allen
Pisasale, Charles
Tully, Paul Gregory

*   *   *

Appendix 4

SOURCE: GLOBAL INFO-LINKS INFORMATION GUIDE 1995

WHO CAN SUBSCRIBE TO GLOBAL INFO-LINKS?

Anyone can become a GIL subscriber! However, it's most economical to join us if you live in the Ipswich Region or Brisbane so that you can access us for the cost of a local telephone call. If you live outside these areas you'll be charged community call or STD rates. Because GIL was established by the Ipswich City Council, Ipswich region residents receive a discount off the normal subscription rates (Ipswich region consists of the Ipswich, Boonah, Laidley, Gatton and Esk local government areas).

NB: If you're concerned that you're not located in a local call area, please contact Telstra on 012 and they'll advise you what call rate will apply. Alternately, you can refer to Telstra's White Pages for locality bands.

WHAT YOU NEED TO GET STARTED:
- Subscription to Global Info-Links
- Personal Computer
- Normal Telephone Line
- Modem
- Printer (optional)

DETAILS OF HARDWARE AND SOFTWARE REQUIREMENTS

IBM Windows Environment (Windows 3.X or Windows 95)

HARDWARE:	MINIMUM:	RECOMMENDED:
Modem	Hayes Compatible (Min. 14.4 kbps)	33.6 kbps
Hard Disk Space	40mByte	80 - 200mByte
RAM	8mByte	16mByte +
Monitor	VGA	SVGA (256 colour)
CPU	486SX 25	Pentium or better

ADDITIONAL HARDWARE REQUIREMENTS:
Telephone outlet
Spare serial communications port (16550 UART recommended)

ADDITIONAL HARDWARE SUGGESTIONS:
Microsoft Windows compatible mouse or other pointing device
Colour or black and white printer
Stereo sound card, speakers and microphone

SOFTWARE SUGGESTIONS:
- Microsoft Internet Explorer
- Microsoft Internet Mail and News
- PPP Modem Dialler and Connection software
- FTP client - WSFTP or CUTEFTP
- Chat client - mIRC or Pirch
- Graphics Viewer - LView
- Telnet client - EWAN or CRT
- Virus Protection - McAfee
- Decompression Utilities – WinZip or PKUnzip

NOTE: Software highlighted by shaded box is supplied by Global Info-Links.

IBM Non-Windows Environment (DOS 3.1 or better)

HARDWARE:	MINIMUM:	RECOMMENDED:
Modem	Hayes Compatible (Min. 2400 bps)	9600 bps or better
Hard Disk Space	2mByte	50mByte
RAM	640kByte	1mByte
Monitor	Any	Colour VGA
CPU	XT (8086)	486 or better

ADDITIONAL HARDWARE REQUIREMENTS:
Telephone outlet
Spare serial communications port

ADDITIONAL HARDWARE SUGGESTIONS: Colour or black and white printer

SOFTWARE SUGGESTIONS: VT100 terminal emulation (e.g. telix)

OTHER COMPUTERS (e.g. AMIGA):
Most support VT100 emulation - using a Hayes compatible modem.

Apple Macintosh and Power PC

HARDWARE:	MINIMUM:	RECOMMENDED:
System	System 7.5.3	System 7.5.5 or better
RAM	8mByte	16mByte +
CPU	68000	68030 PowerMac or better

ADDITIONAL HARDWARE REQUIREMENTS:
Telephone outlet
Spare serial communications port

ADDITIONAL HARDWARE SUGGESTIONS: Colour or black and white printer

OTHER: Macintosh LiveWire! Kit (software only)
Macintosh LiveWire! Kit (software and modem)

SOFTWARE:
The following software will need to be purchased from your local Macintosh retailer.
➤ Apple Internet Connection Kit   ➤ MacTCP and Free PPP
➤ Open Transport and Free PPP   ➤ Microsoft Internet Explorer for Mac
➤ Microsoft Mail and News for Mac

6

Only pay for the time you use!

GIL sells Internet subscriptions as blocks of time. You can buy blocks of time from us that you can use over a month, a quarter, six months or a year – the choice is entirely up to you. And you can use up your time block at your own pace: a little one week, a lot the next. We don't attempt to tie you to any fixed pattern.

If you completely use up a time block before your expiry date, you can simply contact GIL and purchase another one. But if you reach the end of your subscription period and haven't used all your time up, we'll roll over any unused hours into your next subscription if you purchase another time block from us on or before your expiry date. **This unique roll-over facility** – the ability to carry your unused hours from one subscription period to the next – means that all our long-term subscribers only pay for the time they actually use.

ACCESS PROVIDED: Terminal Emulation, Point to Point Protocol (PPP), Serial Line Internet Protocol (SLIP)

SERVICE PROVIDED: Email, Newsgroups, Web Browsing, Gopher Browsing, Telnet, FTP.

HOME PAGE: A personal site for the subscriber.

Ipswich City Council offers to subscribers the ability to create their own home page on the Global Info-Links Web. A Web Page containing information on how to develop the home page is available on the following address:

http://www.gil.com.au/~trainer

This service is only available to Global Info-Links Subscribers and is only to contain personal information (no advertising) created and posted by the subscriber. If you require more personal space there is a charge of $10 per megabyte or part thereof per month, with a maximum of five megabytes imposed. Contact Global Info-Links Administration for more details.

"...the ability to create your own home page..."

SPACE ALLOWED: 2 Megabytes for each user

RESTRICTIONS: No advertising of products and services.
No information contrary to Item 7.2 of the Global Info-Links General Subscriber Agreement.

FOR MORE INFORMATION:
Mail: Global Info-Links Subscriptions, PO Box 191, IPSWICH QLD 4305
Phone: (07) 3810 6787 **Fax:** (07) 3810 6743 **Email:** subs@gil.com.au

7

About the Author:

In the last twenty-five years Mal Bryce has worked as a cabinet minister, company director, corporate manager and senior consultant. During the 1980s he established

- Australia's most successful technology park, at Bentley in Western Australia,
- The Western Australian Small Business Development Corporation,
- The Western Australian SciTech Discovery Centre,
- Australia's first government department of Computing and Information Technology,
- The Institute for Science and Technology Policy and the Chair of Biotechnology at Murdoch University, and
- The public policy that revolutionised regional development in Western Australia.

As Minister for Electoral Reform he was responsible for the passage of the 1987 Reform Bill which produced sweeping changes to the electoral system in Western Australia. Throughout the 1990s Mal was a leading Australian pioneer in the development of the Internet industry and the application of the Internet to business, government agencies and communities. He is a former

- Deputy Premier of Western Australia.
- Director of Bank West.
- Executive Chairman of the Australian Centre for Innovation and International Competitiveness. (University of Sydney)
- Chairman/director of six science based companies based in Australia and the USA.
- Member of the Prime Minister's Science and Engineering Council.
- Management Consultant with Deloitte Ross Tohmatsu.

- Foundation Co-Chairman (1989) of the Australian Greenhouse Information Service (Melbourne)
- Chairman of the Western Australian, Technology and Industry Advisory Council.
- Chairman of the Governing Council of Perth Central TAFE.
- Chairman of the WA. ICT Industry Development Forum.
- Chairman of the WA Tele-Centre Advisory Council.
- Director of Yilgarn Infrastructure Ltd.

After a lifetime of involvement with the ICT revolution and innovation, Mal is a regular keynote speaker and strategist in this field. He was admitted as a Foundation Fellow of the Australian Institute of Company Directors in 1990. He is chairman of iVEC, a senior associate of the Australian Centre for Innovation (Sydney), chairman of the Pawsey Super Computer Project, a member of the Australian eResearch Infrastructure Council and Adjunct Professor of Public Policy at Curtin University.

Index

LaVergne, TN USA
21 January 2011
213507LV00001B/1/P